Susanne Seethaler

Bayerisch süß

Sweet Bavarian Treats

Susanne Seethaler

Bayerisch süß

Sweet Bavarian Treats

Ins Amerikanische übersetzt von Susan Byron

Traditionelle Nachspeisen und feines Gebäck mit Weihnachtsbackteil

Traditional desserts, cakes and cookies including Christmas specialties

nymphenburger

Für meine Schwester Renee
To my sister Renee

MIX
Papier aus verantwortungsvollen Quellen
FSC® C012425

Umschlag: atelier-sanna.com, München
Umschlagmotiv: StockFood, München
Illustrationen: shutterstock und Claudia Sanna, atelier-sanna.com
Fotos innen: S. 2, 3, 8-10, 12–15, 33, 93, 113, 131, 142–145:
shutterstock, München; alle anderen Fotos: StockFood GmbH, München
Satz: EDV-Fotosatz Huber/Verlagsservice G. Pfeifer, Germering
Gesetzt aus 9,8 pt/13 pt Minion Pro
Druck und Binden: Offizin Andersen Nexö, Leipzig
Printed in Germany
ISBN 978-3-485-02826-4

www.nymphenburger-verlag.de

INHALT

CONTENTS

VORWORT

Die Bayern sind ein »süßes« Völkchen, auch wenn in den Köpfen vieler eher ein deftiger Schweinsbraten, eine schaumgekrönte Mass Bier oder mitunter sogar ein fetter Kanten Speck zur Brotzeit mit diesem schönen Land und seinen Ureinwohnern verbunden wird. Aber der Bayer an sich kann eben auch »süß«, davon erzählen nicht umsonst so bekannte Süßspeisen wie der Kaiserschmarrn, die Auszogene oder die Rohrnudel – auch wenn Ersterer genau genommen als weltberühmte Mehlspeise seinen Ursprung im benachbarten Österreich hat. Überhaupt sind die kulinarischen Grenzen zwischen Österreich und Bayern eher fließend, das liegt nicht nur an der geografischen Lage, sondern fußt auch in der Geschichte dieser beiden Nachbarn. So breitete sich das ehemalige Gebiet Altbayerns einst im Osten bis über Linz hinaus aus, um im Süden seine »Fühler« sogar bis nach Bozen, also bis nach Italien hinunter, auszustrecken. Da liegt es nahe, dass sich unter anderem auch die Mehlspeisen der verschiedenen Alpenregionen untereinander vermischten und »süße Ehen« miteinander eingingen.
Eines haben übrigens alle bayerischen Süßigkeiten und Süßspeisen, sei es ein simpler Rührkuchen, die klassische Schmalznudel oder ein verführerisch duftender Zwetschgendatschi, gemeinsam: Sie sind recht einfach in der Herstellung, sieht man mal von den obligatorischen Ausnahmen, die die Regel bestätigen, ab. So braucht es beispielsweise für die »Bayerisch Creme« doch etwas Fingerspitzengefühl, und Hefeteig, z.B. für den klassischen Zopf, ist auf Anhieb auch nicht jedermanns Sache, aber ansonsten können Sie sich ohne Angst an die Rezepte in diesem Buch wagen, denn im Grunde kann nicht viel schiefgehen.

Viele Rezepte stammen aus der bäuerlichen Küche, in der in früheren Zeiten oft Schmalhans regierte. Also musste die Hausfrau mit wenigen Zutaten etwas Leckeres zaubern. Zu-

INTRODUCTION

Bavarians are a "sweet" little people, even though in the minds of many, it is thought that this beautiful country and its local people prefer a hearty pork roast, a foam-crowned mug of beer, or sometimes even bacon fat to the snack on. But the Bavarians themselves can be just as "sweet," as can be seen by their desserts such as the "Kaiserschmarrn," the "Auszogene" or the tube pastry – even if the latter as a world-famous pastry actually originates in the neighboring Austria. However, the culinary borders between Austria and Bavaria are rather fluid, so it is not only based on the geographical location but also on the history of these two neighbors. The former area of old Bavaria reached once into the East via Linz; in the South it extended as far as Bolzano, and after Italy, a sort of "feelers" stretch out to capture culinary impressions. Since it's clear that these countries' dishes have mingled, the pastries from various Alpine regions are known as "sweet marriages."

All Bavarian sweets and common desserts, such as a simple sponge cake, the classic lard noodle or a seductively fragrant "Zwetschgendatschi" are quite simple to make, apart from the typical exceptions to the rule. So, for example, all that is needed for "Bavarian cream" is some yeast dough and tact. For the classic braid, a little more skill is required and not everyone succeeds right off the bat, but otherwise, you can confidently explore and experiment with the various recipes in this book because basically not much can go wrong.

Many recipes come from peasant cuisine, which in the past was often more popular. So the housewife with only a few ingredients had to somehow conjure up something delicious. Sugar was also often scarce and too expensive for many households. On fast days, when meat and fish were forbidden by the Catholic Church, the sweet – but also hefty – pastries, such as steam pastry, were supposed to bolster the hard

cker war zudem oft rar und für viele Haushalte einfach zu teuer. An Fastentagen, an denen Fleisch und Fisch tabu waren und die es in der katholischen Kirche bis heute reichlich gibt, sollten die süßen – aber auch deftigen – Mehlspeisen, wie Dampfnudeln oder Schmarrn, auch noch für die harte Arbeit auf dem Hof satt machen. Kein leichtes Unterfangen. Und so backte die findige Bäuerin ihre Teignudeln und -taschen eben kurzerhand im triefenden Fett heraus, damit die Männer stark genug blieben für Feld und Stall. Das traditionelle Schmalzgebäck in seinen verschiedenen Formen bildet bis in unsere heutige Zeit hinein aber auch eine, rein magentechnisch gesehen, willkommene Grundlage auf diversen Festen, wo Bier und Schnaps in der Regel in Strömen fließen. Aber das ist eine andere Geschichte, die wir hier nicht vertiefen wollen. Denken Sie bei Ihrem nächsten Oktoberfestbesuch einfach daran: So eine Auszogene kann Wunder wirken, wenn Sie sich entschließen, tief ins Glas bzw. in den Bierkrug zu blicken.

Viele Süßspeisen sind in Bayern auch mit hohen Kirchentagen, den sogenannten »Hochfesten«, verbunden. So isst man in manchen Gebieten des Freistaats heute noch Kirchweihnudeln eben ausschließlich an Kirchweih, und die zugegebenermaßen geschmacklich etwas gewöhnungsbedürftigen Schux'n haben am Dreikönigstag ihren großen Auftritt. Selbstredend sind Weihnachtsplätzchen, Kletzenbrot und Co. der Advents- und Weihnachtszeit vorbehalten, und an Ostern erfreut sich Groß und Klein natürlich am Osterbrot, das vor dem Verzehr feierlich in der Kirche geweiht wird.

Die Bayern sind im Grunde durch und durch Genussmenschen, und diese Eigenschaft macht auch vor der nachmittäglichen Kaffeetafel nicht halt. Kuchen aller Art sind in ganz Bayern sehr beliebt. Lediglich auf die Nachspeise, also das Dessert, verzichtet so manch bayerisches und überwiegend männliches Urgestein gerne zugunsten eines kräftigen Schnapses. In dieser Sache ist dieses Völkchen halt eigen – wie in so manch anderen Dingen auch –, aber genau das macht den Menschenschlag nördlich der Alpen weit über die Grenzen ihres Landes hinweg so beliebt.

workers in the fields. Not an easy task. And so, the resourceful farmers baked their dough noodles and put them in bags drizzling with fat, so that the men could maintain their strength to work in the fields and barns. Nowadays, the traditional cakes in their various forms are based on various festivals, often where beer and liquor are flowing generously. But that's another story all together, we don't want to go into here. Just remember this during your next visit to Oktoberfest: an "Auszogene" can work wonders if you decide to 'peer a bit too deeply' into the glass or the beer mug as they say with a wink in Germany.

Many sweets are also linked to the High Church, its so-called "feast days," in Bavaria, Germany. So today, "Kirchweih" noodles are eaten solely to bless some areas of the state, and the "Schux'n" make their grand entrance during the Epiphany. Obviously, Christmas cookies, bread from dried pears and Co are reserved for Advent and the Christmas season, and during Easter, large and small Easter breads are enjoyed, having been solemnly blessed in the Church before being eaten.

The Bavarians are thoroughly sensual and know how to truly enjoy life, including their rich afternoon coffee rituals. Cakes of all kinds are very popular in Bavaria. Many Bavarians, however, especially "the old Geezers" will gladly exchange their treats for a sweet brandy. These people are just intrinsically particular – as is the case in so many other areas –, yet it is largely this obstinate originality that makes this breed north of the Alps so endearing and popular far beyond their own borders.

Some baking books are prefaced with an intimidating claim that "Baking is a skill that needs to be learned and earned." Now, let me reveal a little secret: I, probably together with many of you, dear readers, have also not learned to bake professionally. I simply work twice a week in a small Munich

In manchen Backbüchern steht gleich im Vorwort ein, wie ich finde etwas beängstigender, Hinweis, der da lautet »Backen will gelernt sein!«. Nun, dazu kann ich Ihnen gleich ein kleines Geheimnis anvertrauen, das ich vermutlich mit vielen von Ihnen, liebe Leser und Leserinnen, gemeinsam habe: Ich habe das Backen auch nicht professionell erlernt. Ich arbeite zweimal die Woche in einem kleinen Münchner Café als Köchin, die Backschichten übernehmen pfiffige – ungelernte! – Studentinnen, die nach den Rezeptanweisungen unserer Chefin jeden Tag ein bisschen mehr dazulernen. Trotzdem, oder vielleicht gerade deswegen, sind wir in ganz München bekannt und beliebt wegen unserer Kuchen, Tartes und süßen Köstlichkeiten.
Also: Ausrede gilt nicht! Haben Sie Spaß am Backen und am Zubereiten all der anderen wunderbar süßen Köstlichkeiten, die ich für Sie im Bekannten- und Freundeskreis, bei meiner Mutter und auf so manch abgelegenem Bauernhof recherchiert habe.
Übrigens, über ein halbes Jahr lang bin ich fast täglich in meiner kleinen Küche gestanden und habe die gesammelten Rezepte auf Ihre Tauglichkeit getestet. Manchmal musste ich mehrfach ran, weil der Hefeteig beim ersten Mal nicht aufging, ich das Backpulver vergessen hatte oder weil meine Bayerisch Creme nicht fest wurde. Oder das Spritzgebäck: Der Teig aus dem ersten Rezept, das ich von einer Freundin meiner Mutter hatte, war so fest wie Stein. Als ich versuchte, ihn durch die Spritztülle zu drücken, brach ich mir fast das Handgelenk. Erst das zweite Rezept, von einem befreundeten Profikoch, funktionierte auf Anhieb.
Sie sehen schon, ich habe während dieser Zeit unendlich viel gelernt … und meine Nachbarn, denen ich in meiner Not und in Ermangelung einer großen Gefriertruhe alles zum Verkosten vor die Türe gestellt habe, sind in den letzten Monaten wohl ein bisschen fülliger geworden. »Backen will also doch gelernt sein«, aber man oder frau kann es wirklich sehr schnell erlernen.

Ich wünsche Ihnen genauso viel Freude beim Ausprobieren, wie ich sie hatte!

Café as a cook, whereas the bake shifts are filled by smart, but unskilled students, who learn a little bit more every day just by following our boss's instructions. Nevertheless, or perhaps because of this, we are known and loved all over Munich for our cakes, tarts and "Nun's Farts" which we have politely retitled "Puffs" in this book.

So, no excuses! Have fun baking and making all the other wonderful sweet treats, which I have collected for you among my circle of friends and acquaintances, from my mother and discovered in many far-flung, secluded farms.
Incidentally, for almost half a year, almost daily, I sorted these recipes in my small kitchen and then tested them for their suitability. Sometimes I had to repeat these tests several times because initially the yeast dough did not work out for me: I either forgot the baking powder or my Bavarian cream was not stiff enough, or the shortbread cookies were a disaster. The dough from the first recipe gotten from my mother's friend was hard as a rock. When I tried to push it through the nozzle, I practically fractured my wrist. A friendly professional chef recommended a second recipe which worked "right off the batter" – so to speak.

So, you can see I learned a lot during this time ... and my neighbors put on a lot of weight. I used to place little presents before their doors since I didn't have a freezer to store all my delicious experiments. And I needed taste testers and feedback. So, yes, "baking is a skill that has to be learned" and takes some dedication; but actually, it can be learned rather quickly.

I hope you enjoy learning and performing this tasty skill as much as I did.

Zubereitungshinweise

Alle Rezepte sind, wenn nicht anders angegeben, für vier Personen berechnet.

BACKPULVER: Neben dem üblichen Backpulver hat sich auch Weinsteinpulver (aus dem Naturkostladen), das ebenfalls in praktischen kleinen Päckchen portioniert ist, bewährt.

EIER: Wenn nicht anders angegeben, werden stets mittelgroße Eier für die Rezepte verwendet. Es versteht sich von selbst, dass zum Backen stets frische Eier verwendet werden; das ist beim Backen besonders wichtig.
Manche Konditoren schwören bei Eischnee auf eine Rührzeit, bzw. »Schlagzeit«, von mindestens sieben Minuten, inklusive der obligatorischen Prise Salz, die einen besonders festen Eischnee garantiert.

HEFETEIG: Der Hefeteig ist für viele Hobbybäcker und -bäckerinnen ein rotes Tuch, dabei ist Hefe an sich nur eine wimmelnde Ansammlung von Kleinstlebewesen – der Gattung Pilze zugeordnet –, die mit Liebe und Vorsicht behandelt werden wollen, wie alle anderen Lebewesen auch! Sie wollen im Grunde nur eines: fressen. Sie lieben alles, was süß ist, und sie mögen es behaglich warm, während sie reinhauen, was das Zeug hält – zu viel Zucker bekommt ihnen allerdings nicht. Zugluft ist ihnen ein Graus. Wenn Sie es schaffen, die passenden Rahmenbedingungen für Ihre Hefetierchen herzustellen, dann beginnen sie fröhlich zu verdauen – und ihre »Gase« bewirken dann das ersehnte Aufgehen des Teigs.
Wenden Sie Sorgfalt und Fingerspitzengefühl also schon beim sogenannten »Dampferl«, dem Vorteig, an und behandeln Sie Ihre Hefe wie ein Kleinkind, das mit einer Süßigkeit verwöhnt werden möchte, in seinem zarten Alter jedoch selbst noch nicht weiß, was und wie viel ihm guttut. Halten Sie also Maß in Sachen Zucker und gehen Sie ohne Angst ran an die Hefe, dann kann nichts schiefgehen.

Hier noch mal die Hauptgründe, warum Ihr Hefeteig vielleicht nicht aufgegangen ist:

- Die Hefe war nicht mehr frisch genug.
- Der Teig hat an einem Ort geruht, der nicht warm genug oder zu zugig war. Oder der Ort war zu warm – z. B. im Backrohr. Bei über 50 Grad stirbt die Hefe.

Preparation Instructions

All recipes are in metric weights and can be converted to US volume standards using a variety of online conversion programs; however, it should be noted that converting from weight to volume depends on the density of the substance. Another option is to use a converter measuring glass.
You can make your own vanilla sugar: Split the pod of the vanilla bean, scrape out the seeds and let pod dry. Combine with sugar in an airtight jar and you will always have a supply of vanilla sugar on hand. Should the aroma become too intense in time, simply remove the bean. As a rule of thumb, the more beans there are, the stronger the vanilla flavor and the aroma will be.
Unless otherwise stated, all recipes are for four people.

TARTAR POWDER has proven to be a good substitute for baking powder and can be purchased in Health Food stores, which also offers it in convenient, smaller units.

EGGS: Unless otherwise indicated, the medium sized eggs are always used in the recipes. It goes without saying that for baking, fresh eggs are always used, which is particularly important during baking.
Some pastry chefs swear by egg whites mixed for at least seven minutes ("stiffening time"), including the obligatory pinch of salt, which guarantees a particularly firm meringue.

YEAST DOUGH: For many home bakers and cooks, the idea of working with yeast dough is a source of some concern, yet yeast is really, simply just a teeming collection of micro-organisms – assigned to the fungi family – who only need and want to be treated with love and care, like all other living creatures. Basically, they only want to do one thing: eat. They love anything that is sweet, and they like it warm and cozy – but be careful: they will go crazy if they get too much sugar. And they hate drafts. If you can manage to create the right environment for these little creatures, after gobbling up and digesting their sugar, they will reward you with lots of fabulous, little farts, causing the dough to rise. These prized little pockets of gas push and fluff up the dough. If you treat these creatures with the same affection and care as you would a child, who only wants to be catered to and given lots of sweets but doesn't know when enough is enough, then your so-called "Dampferl," the pre-dough, will be more than happy to plump up and

* Die Hefe ist im Vorteig mit Salz oder mit Fett (z. B. zerlassene Butter) in Berührung gekommen. Das absolute »No-Go« für diese Schleckermäulchen. Übrigens, am besten ist es, wenn Sie Butter und Salz beim Verkneten des Hefeteigs – falls die beiden im Rezept stehen – ganz zum Schluss unterkneten. Das ist zwar ein bisschen mühsam, aber es garantiert ein sicheres Aufgehen des Teigs.
* Der Teig hat nicht lange genug geruht.
* Der Teig wurde nicht lange genug geknetet.
* Milch oder Wasser zum Anrühren des Vorteigs waren zu heiß.
* Im Teig ist zu viel Zucker.

Tipps:

* Manche Menschen schwören darauf, den fertigen Hefeteig immer wieder auf der Arbeitsfläche »abzuschlagen«, damit Luft in den Teig kommt, bevor er im Ofen gebacken wird. Die Meinungen darüber gehen allerdings auseinander. Ich selbst schlage mal, mal schlage ich nicht ... je nach Gemütsverfassung. Das Ergebnis war bisher, so oder so, immer zufriedenstellend.
* Bei allen Rezepten in diesem Buch können Sie natürlich auch Trockenhefe verwenden, was das Backergebnis in keinster Weise negativ beeinflusst. Verfahren Sie einfach nach der jeweiligen Packungsanleitung.
* Faustregel: 20 g frische Hefe entsprechen 1 Päckchen Trockenhefe. 1 Päckchen Trockenhefe ist ausreichend für 500 g Mehl.

HITZE: Wenn nicht anders angegeben: Ober- und Unterhitze, mittlere Schiene
Und nicht vergessen: Jeder Herd ist anders! Hitze und Zubereitungszeit können also von Backrohr zu Backrohr variieren.

MEHL: Wenn nicht anders angegeben: Weizenmehl Type 405

MENGENANGABEN: Falls nicht anders angegeben, handelt sich bei den Löffelmaßeinheiten immer um gestrichene Tee- bzw. Esslöffel der jeweiligen Zutaten.

MILCH: Manche Rezepte verlangen explizit nach Vollmilch (zuweilen sogar frisch vom Bauernhof) – sonst aber können Sie auch Milch mit geringerem Fettanteil verwenden.

please you. So, if you do not use too much sugar, then you don't need to worry about your yeast dough failing.

Here are the main reasons why your dough might not rise:

* The yeast was not fresh enough.
* The dough rested in a place that was either not warm enough or too drafty. Or the place was too warm. Even at only 120°F the yeast will begin to die.
* The yeast in the dough has come into contact with salt or fat (e.g. melted butter). These are an absolute "no-go" for these tots. If the two are in the recipe – kneading them into the risen yeast dough at the end is the best way when you are using butter and salt. Although this is a bit of a chore, it guarantees a sure dough rise.
* The dough has not rested long enough.
* The dough was not kneaded long enough.
* The milk or water to mix the pre-dough was too hot.
* The dough has too much sugar.

Tips & Hints

* Some people swear by it when the finished dough is repeatedly "thrown" or "slapped" on the work surface, so that air comes into the dough before it is baked. However, opinions about this differ. I suggest doing it at times but not always ... depending on the mood. Either way, so far, the result has always been satisfactory.
* You can also use dry yeast with all the recipes in this book, which does not negatively affect the baking results in any way. Process it by following the package instructions.
* Rule of thumb: 1 envelope or sachet dry yeast (1/4 oz) = 2 1/4 teaspoons = 1 cake fresh yeast (3/5 oz), which is sufficient for 500 g flour or roughly 4 cups.

HEAT: Unless stated otherwise: top and bottom heat, use middle rack. Do not forget: Every oven is different. Heating and baking time can, therefore, vary from oven to oven.

FLOUR: Unless otherwise indicated: Wheat flour type 405

QUANTITIES: Unless otherwise indicated, are standard tea- or tablespoon units, always leveled.

MILK: Some recipes explicitly call for whole milk (sometimes even fresh from the farm) – but, otherwise, you can use milk with lower fat content.

STÄBCHENPROBE: Stechen Sie gegen Ende der Backzeit mit einem langen hölzernen Spießchen in die Kuchenmasse. Bleiben Teigreste daran hängen, ist der Kuchen noch nicht gar und braucht noch etwas mehr Zeit im Ofen.

WASSERBAD: Für ein Wasserbad erhitzen Sie etwas Wasser in einem kleinen Topf, auf dem Sie bequem eine etwas größere Porzellan- oder Steingutschüssel, in die Sie die grob zerkleinerte Schokolade geben, platzieren können, ohne dass der Boden der Schüssel die Wasseroberfläche berührt. Lediglich der Wasserdampf soll die Schokolade zum Schmelzen bringen.

WEIHNACHTSPLÄTZCHEN: Meine Mutter gibt in die Vorratsdosen mit den Plätzchen manchmal einen kleinen Apfelschnitz – so bleibt das Weihnachtsgebäck schön saftig. Grundsätzlich gilt für die Lagerung: gut verschließbare Dosen und ein kühler Ort, denn sonst werden die Plätzchen schnell hart.

ZUCKER: Versuchen Sie es beim Backen mal mit »Extrafeinem Backzucker«, der macht Ihre Kuchen und süßen Leckereien tatsächlich und im wahrsten Sinne des Wortes noch »feiner«. Eine gute Alternative zu herkömmlichem Zucker ist auch Puderzucker. Herkömmlicher Zucker löst sich, ebenso wie brauner Zucker, im Teig nicht so gut auf.
Als gesündere, dunkle Varianten gelten Brauner Rohzucker, Vollrohrzucker und Muscovadozucker. Die meisten Rezepte in diesem Buch sind allerdings sehr alt, sodass so gut wie immer auf herkömmlichen weißen Zucker zurückgegriffen wird. Brauner Zucker verleiht den Backwaren einen karamelligen Geschmack.

ZU GUTER LETZT: Lesen Sie sich das jeweilige Rezept einmal komplett durch, bevor Sie loslegen. So bekommen Sie einen ersten Überblick über die Arbeitsabläufe und erleben keine bösen Überraschungen, wie z. B. das Vergessen des Backpulvers oder einer anderen wichtigen Zutat, wie es mir zuweilen schon passiert ist.

SKEWER TEST: Insert a long wooden skewer into the cake mixture towards the end of the baking time. Dough residue will stick to the skewer when the cake is not completely cooked and still needs some more time in the oven.

WATER BATH: For a water bath, heat up some water in a small pot which you can easily place a slightly larger porcelain or earthenware bowl on top of, into which coarsely chopped chocolate is filled, making sure the bottom of the bowl does not touch the water surface. Only the steam is needed to melt the chocolate.

CHRISTMAS COOKIES: My mother sometimes left a small wedge of apple in the storage jars with cookies – so the Christmas cakes stayed nice and juicy. Basic for storage: tightly sealable containers, usually tins with lids, and a cool place to prevent the cookies from becoming stale too quickly.

SUGAR: Try baking with "extra fine baking sugar." It actually and literally makes your cakes and sweet treats "extra fine." A good alternative to conventional sugar is powdered sugar. Conventional sugar does not dissolve as well in the dough as it is not as high quality as brown sugar.
As a healthier option, you can use dark brown raw sugar variants, whole cane sugar and Muscovado sugar. However, most of the recipes in this book are very old, so you can always use conventional white sugar. Brown sugar gives baked goods a caramel flavor.

CURD CHEESE ("QUARK"): The "Quark" used in Germany is a mild, creamy fresh cheese, which is not matured. Usually, it is available in a substantial variation (40% fat in dry measure) and a lean version (20% fat in dry measure). Although it differs from cottage cheese and ricotta it can easily be replaced if "Quark" is not available in your local supermarket, usually with one of these products. If you prefer, cottage cheese or ricotta can be whipped in a blender to remove the grainy lumps and create a creamier texture more like "Quark."

FINALLY: Always read each recipe completely once through before you get started, so you have an initial overview of the worksteps and can avoid any nasty surprises, such as forgetting the baking powder or other important ingredients.

Süße Aufläufe - In der Bratreine gebacken

Baked Goods – Prepared in a Casserole Dish

Süße Aufläufe haben in der ländlichen Küche Bayerns Tradition. Das katholische Kirchenjahr wartet mit recht vielen Fastentagen auf, auf die in manchen Gegenden heute noch Rücksicht genommen wird. So ist z. B. auch der Freitag auf vielen Bauerhöfen nach wie vor ein Tag, an dem kein Fleisch auf den Tisch kommt.

Cakes, tarts, and pies are part of a long tradition in Bavarian country cuisine. In many regions today, the many fasting days of the Catholic Church are still adhered to. Therefore, on many farms today, as it was back then, meat is not served on Fridays.

APRIKOSEN IM POLENTABETT

Zubereitungszeit inkl. Backzeit ca. 45 Minuten

Polenta, also Maisgrieß, ist eher im südlichen Alpengebiet bekannt – im ursprünglichen Rezept, das von einer Bäuerin nördlich der Alpen stammt, wird ganz normaler Weizengrieß angegeben. Mir persönlich schmeckt allerdings diese Variante besser. Probieren Sie bei Gelegenheit beides aus.

ZUTATEN

600 ml Milch
100 g Maisgrieß (Polenta)
2 TL (1 Pck.) Vanillezucker
1 EL Zucker
1 Prise Salz
abgeriebene Schale von 1 unbehandelten Orange
wahlweise 1 Prise gemahlener Kurkuma – gar nicht bayerisch, aber es unterstützt die Gelbfärbung der Polenta so schön
3 Eigelb
3 Eiweiß, mit 1 Prise Salz zu Eischnee geschlagen
750 g Aprikosen, gewaschen, halbiert und entkernt

AUSSERDEM 1 Auflaufform, Butter zum Einfetten der Form, 50 g Mandelblättchen, in der Pfanne trocken geröstet

ZUBEREITUNG

Milch in einem Topf aufkochen lassen. Polenta, Vanillezucker, Zucker und Salz zugeben und unter ständigem Rühren zu einem dicken Brei kochen. Orangenabrieb und evtl. etwas gemahlenen Kurkuma unterrühren, dann beiseitestellen und auskühlen lassen.

BAKED APRICOT POLENTA CAKE

Preparation time including baking time approx. 45 minutes

Polenta, also called cornmeal, is more widespread in the Southern Alpine regions. The original recipe, which was acquired from a farmer in the Northern Alps, used wheat semolina instead of cornmeal. I personally prefer the recipe like this, but you should try out both when you have the time.

INGREDIENTS

2 1/2 cups milk
3 1/2 oz polenta
2 tsp (1 sachet) vanilla sugar
1 Tb sugar
1 pinch salt
grated rind of 1 orange
optional: 1 pinch turmeric (while not at all Bavarian, it is, however, great for giving a beautiful yellow tint to the polenta)
3 egg yolks
3 egg whites, add 1 pinch salt and beat until frothy/stiff
4 cups apricots, washed and pitted

IN ADDITION 1 casserole dish, butter for greasing, 1/4 cup almond flakes, roasted in a pan

METHOD

Bring milk to a boil. Add polenta, vanilla sugar, sugar and salt. While stirring, continue to cook until it turns into a thick porridge. Add the ground orange rind and – if desired – turmeric and mix. Set aside and let cool.

Eigelbe in einer Schüssel schaumig schlagen und unter den erkalteten Polentabrei rühren. Dann Eischnee unterziehen und die Masse gleichmäßig in die eingefettete Auflaufform füllen.
Backofen auf 180 Grad vorheizen.
Aprikosenhälften auf der Polenta verteilen und den Auflauf ca. 30 Minuten im Ofen backen. Zum Servieren mit gerösteten Mandelblättchen bestreuen.

When the polenta porridge has completely cooled, beat the egg yolks in a bowl until stiff and mix in. Then fold in the frothy egg whites and pour into the casserole dish.
Preheat oven to 350°F.
Arrange the apricot halves on top of the polenta and bake for approximately 30 minutes. Sprinkle with roasted almond flakes before serving.

Tipps

* *Schmeckt auch prima mit Hirsebrei! Garnieren Sie das Ganze zusätzlich mit gerösteten Kokosflocken, das ist zwar auch nicht sehr bayerisch, schmeckt aber toll.*
* *Diesen Auflauf kann man auch gut zum Frühstück servieren.*

Tips & Hints

* *Try the recipe using millet gruel instead of polenta. You can also sprinkle with roasted coconut flakes when serving. This is not very Bavarian but very delicious.*
* *This cake can be served for a wonderful breakfast.*

HERZENSWÄRMER MIT HIMBEEREN

Zubereitungszeit inkl. Backzeit ca. 1 Stunde 15 Minuten

Trübsal und Liebeskummer, Herzweh und Seelennot, das kennen natürlich auch die Bayern; davor bleibt kein Mensch gefeit. Da kommt dieser »Herzenswärmer« gerade recht. Das Rezept vereint sämig süßen Milchreis mit Quark und Himbeeren und lässt wenigstens für eine kurze Zeit alle Sorgen vergessen.

ZUTATEN

1 l Vollmilch
ca. 60 g Butter
Abrieb und Saft von 1 unbehandelten Zitrone
80 g Zucker
250 g Milchreis, gewaschen
1 Msp. Zimtpulver
500 g Magerquark, 20% Fett i. Tr.
3 Eigelb
300 g Himbeeren, tiefgefroren
3 Eiweiß, mit 1 Prise Salz steif geschlagen

AUSSERDEM 1 Auflaufform

ZUBEREITUNG

Milch, Butter, Zitronenabrieb, Zitronensaft und Zucker in einen Topf geben und aufkochen lassen. Milchreis einrühren und auf kleiner Flamme unter ständigem Rühren zu einem Brei einkochen. Zum Schluss Zimtpulver unterrühren. Kurz beiseitestellen.
Backofen auf 180 Grad vorheizen.
Magerquark in eine Schüssel geben. Eigelbe und gefrorene Himbeeren unterrühren. Die Quarkmasse anschließend mit dem warmen Milchreis vermengen. Dann den Eischnee unterrühren. Die Masse in eine ungefettete Auflaufform füllen und im Ofen ca. 50 Minuten backen, bis eine goldgelbe Kruste entsteht.
Der Herzenswärmer schmeckt warm ebenso gut wie kalt aus dem Kühlschrank.

Tipp Zum Herzenswärmer passen Beeren aller Art.

HEART WARMER

(RASPBERRY CAKE IN A CASSEROLE DISH)

Preparation time including baking time approx. 1 hour 15 minutes

Heartbreak, pain and sorrow, desperation and grief, things that every Bavarian knows just as well as the rest of us. Which is when this "heart warmer" comes in handy. This recipe combines smooth, sweet rice pudding with curd cheese and raspberries, leading to delicious oblivion.

INGREDIENTS

4 1/4 cups whole milk
approx. 4 Tb butter
grated rind of 1 lemon
1/3 cup sugar
1 cup round rice for rice pudding, washed
1 scant tsp cinnamon powder
2 cups low-fat curd cheese
3 egg yolks
3 cups frozen raspberries
3 egg whites, add 1 pinch salt and beat until stiff

IN ADDITION 1 casserole dish

METHOD

Place milk, butter, grated lemon rind, lemon juice and sugar in a pot and bring to a boil. Add rice pudding and while continually stirring, keep on a low flame until it is boiled down to a porridge. Lastly add cinnamon powder. Set aside.
Preheat oven to 350°F.
Place curd cheese in a bowl and stir in the egg yolks and frozen raspberries. Then add it to the (still) warm rice porridge. Fold in frothy egg whites and pour into the ungreased casserole dish. Bake for approximately 50 minutes until a golden crust appears. The "Herzenswärmer" (heart warmer) is a delight when served hot, straight from the oven, or cold, after having been refrigerated.

Tips & Hints If you want to mix it up, try this recipe with any kind of berry.

KUCHENMICHL MIT ÄPFELN

Zubereitungszeit ca. 15 Minuten + 15 Minuten Ruhezeit für den Teig + Backzeit 40–45 Minuten

Der Kuchenmichl ist ein uraltes bäuerliches Rezept aus der Alpenregion. In früheren Jahren kam dieser einfache, süße Auflauf, noch warm aus dem Ofen, mitsamt der Bratreine auf den Tisch. Löffel wurden verteilt und jeder, Bauernfamilie und Bedienstete gleichermaßen, bediente sich direkt aus der Form.

ZUTATEN

FÜR DEN TEIG

150 g Mehl
250 ml Milch
3 Eier
1 EL Zucker
2 TL (1 Pck.) Vanillezucker
1/2 TL Salz

AUSSERDEM 3 große säuerliche Äpfel, z. B. Elstar oder Cox Orange, geschält, vom Kerngehäuse befreit und in feine Scheiben geschnitten, Butter zum Einfetten der Auflaufform, 2–3 EL Zucker, 1/2 TL Zimt

ZUBEREITUNG

Alle Zutaten für den Teig in einer großen Schüssel gut miteinander verrühren; die Konsistenz des Teigs sollte feinporig und eher flüssig sein. Anschließend beiseitestellen, mit einem Küchentuch abdecken und ca. 15 Minuten ruhen lassen.
Das Backrohr auf 180 Grad vorheizen und die Auflaufform gut mit Butter einfetten. Zimt und Zucker in einem Schüsselchen miteinander verrühren und beiseitestellen.
Dann den Teig in die eingefettete Form geben und die Äpfel gleichmäßig darauf verteilen.
Das Ganze ca. 40–45 Minuten im Rohr goldgelb backen. Noch warm großzügig mit dem Zimt- und Zuckergemisch bestreuen. Sofort servieren.

Tipp Der Kuchenmichl schmeckt auch sehr gut mit Himbeeren, Birnen oder entsteinten Zwetschgen oder Kirschen.

APPLE CAKE

Preparation time approx. 15 minutes + 15 minutes resting time + baking time 40–45 minutes

The "Kuchenmichl" is an ancient peasant recipe from the Alpine region. Back then, this simple, sweet casserole was served fresh from the oven still in the casserole dish. Everyone at the table, the family and servants of the farm, got a spoon and ate directly from the dish.

INGREDIENTS

FOR THE DOUGH

1 1/5 cups flour
1 cup milk
3 eggs
1 Tb sugar
2 tsp (1 sachet) vanilla sugar
1/2 tsp salt

IN ADDITION 3 large tart apples such as Elstar or Cox Orange, peeled, cored and finely sliced, butter for greasing the casserole dish, 2–3 Tb sugar, 1/2 tsp cinnamon

METHOD

Combine all the ingredients in a bowl and mix into a smooth batter. The consistency should be rather runny. Cover with a kitchen towel and set aside for approximately 15 minutes.
Preheat oven to 350°F.
Generously grease the casserole dish. Mix the cinnamon and sugar in a separate bowl and set aside. Pour the batter into the dish and evenly arrange the apples on the surface. Bake for approximately 40–45 minutes until golden. Sprinkle generously with the cinnamon-sugar mixture while still hot and serve immediately.

Tips & Hints Try this cake recipe with raspberries, pears, pitted plums or cherries instead of apples. It's absolutely delicious.

KIRSCHAUFLAUF

Zubereitungszeit ca. 20 Minuten + Backzeit ca. 45–60 Minuten

ZUTATEN

750 g Kirschen, entsteint
1/8 l Wasser
40 g Zucker
2–3 EL Mandelblättchen
100 g Sahne

FÜR DEN TEIG

80 g Butter, zimmerwarm
50 g Zucker
3 Eigelb
3 Eiweiß
100 g Mehl
1/8 l Milch
Abrieb von 1 unbehandelten Zitrone

AUSSERDEM Butter zum Einfetten der Auflaufform

ZUBEREITUNG

Kirschen mit Wasser und Zucker in einen Topf geben und ca. 5 Minuten köcheln lassen. Anschließend in ein Sieb geben. Eine Auflaufform gut mit Butter einfetten und die abgetropften Kirschen darin verteilen. Mandelblättchen und Sahne darübergeben.
Den Backofen auf 180 Grad vorheizen.
Für den Teig Butter und Zucker schaumig schlagen und nach und nach die drei Eigelbe unterrühren; Eiweiß in einer extra Schüssel steif schlagen. Wenn Sie eine Prise Salz oder einen Spritzer Zitrone zum Eiweiß geben, wird der Eischnee fester. Eischnee beiseitestellen.
Zur Schaummasse abwechselnd Mehl und Milch langsam zugeben und unterrühren. Dann den Zitronenabrieb unterheben.
Zum Schluss Eischnee unter die Teigmasse ziehen und über die Kirschen geben. Den Auflauf ca. 45–60 Minuten im Backrohr goldgelb backen.

CHERRY CAKE

Preparation time approx. 20 minutes + baking time approx. 45–60 minutes

INGREDIENTS

1 1/2 lbs pitted cherries
1/2 cup water
1 1/2 Tb sugar
2–3 Tb almond flakes
scant 1/2 cup cream

FOR THE DOUGH

5 1/2 Tb butter at room temperature
3 Tb sugar
3 egg yolks
3 egg whites
4/5 cup flour
1/2 cup milk
grated lemon rind of 1 lemon

IN ADDITION butter for greasing

METHOD

Place cherries, water and sugar in a pot and let simmer for about 5 minutes and then drain. Generously grease the casserole dish with butter and distribute the drained cherries in it. Pour the cream into the dish and also add the almond flakes. Preheat oven to 350°F.
For the actual dough, stir the butter and sugar until foamy. One by one add the 3 egg yolks; continually stirring. In a separate bowl, beat the egg whites until stiff. If you add a pinch of salt or a splash of lemon juice, it will become even stiffer. Set aside.
Take turns adding the flour and milk to the butter-sugar-foam and gently stir in. Fold in the grated lemon rind. Then fold in the frothy egg whites, stir in the cherries and bake cherry cake for about 45–60 minutes until golden.

ROHRNUDELN MIT MOHNFÜLLUNG

Ergibt ca. 12–14 Stück – Zubereitungszeit inkl. Gehzeiten für den Teig ca. 1 Stunde + ca. 30 Minuten Backzeit

Die Rohrnudel ist eine enge Verwandte der Dampfnudel (s. S. 101) und in Bayern ein klassisches Gebäck zum Nachmittagskaffee.

ZUTATEN

FÜR DEN VORTEIG

30 g Hefe
3 EL lauwarme Milch
1 Prise Zucker
ca. 1–2 EL Mehl

FÜR DIE FÜLLUNG

1/8 l Milch
1 Msp. Zimtpulver
125 g Graumohn, gemahlen
50 g Zucker
1 EL Semmelbrösel

FÜR DEN TEIG

500 g Mehl
3 Eier
1 EL zerlassene Butter
1/2 TL Zitronenschalenabrieb
1 Prise Salz

AUSSERDEM 100 g zerlassene Margarine + 1 TL Zucker für die Bratreine

ZUBEREITUNG

Zuerst die Mohnfüllung zubereiten, damit sie auskühlen kann. Dazu Milch in einen Topf geben und mit Zimt aufkochen lassen. Graumohn, Zucker und Semmelbrösel zugeben und unter ständigem Rühren nochmals aufkochen lassen. Die Masse wird recht dick. Vom Herd nehmen und beiseitestellen.
Die Zutaten für den Vorteig, das sogenannte »Dampferl«, in eine Schüssel geben und gut miteinander verrühren. Zugedeckt an einem warmen, nicht zugigen Ort 15–20 Minuten gehen lassen.

YEAST CAKE WITH POPPY SEED FILLING

Yields 12–14 cakes – Preparation time including resting time for the dough 1 hour + 30 minutes baking time

It is a close relative of the "Dampfnudel" (see pg. 101) and baked until golden brown and crispy. "Rohrnudeln" and coffee are a Bavarian afternoon classic.

INGREDIENTS

FOR THE YEAST STARTER

1/4 cup yeast
3 Tb lukewarm milk
1 pinch salt
approx. 1–2 Tb flour

FOR THE FILLING

1/2 cup milk
1 small pinch ground cinnamon
1/2 cup poppy seeds, ground
3 1/2 Tb sugar
1 Tb dried breadcrumbs

FOR THE DOUGH

4 cups flour
3 eggs
1 Tb melted butter
1/2 tsp grated lemon rind
1 pinch salt

IN ADDITION 1/3 cup melted margarine, 1 tsp sugar for the roasting pan

METHOD

First prepare the poppy seed filling so that it can cool. Put the milk and cinnamon into a saucepan and bring to the boil. Add ground poppy seeds, sugar and breadcrumbs. While constantly stirring, let it come to a boil once more. It will become rather firm and thick. Remove from heat and set aside.
Mix the ingredients for the yeast starter, called "Dampferl," thoroughly in a bowl; cover and place in a warm spot where there is no draft for about 15–20 minutes.
Add the remaining ingredients for the dough in the order listed and knead. Cover and let rise for about 1 hour.

Anschließend die restlichen Zutaten für den Teig zum Vorteig geben und unterkneten. Nochmals zugedeckt ca. 1 Stunde gehen lassen.
Zerlassene Margarine und Zucker miteinander verrühren und in die Bratreine füllen, sodass der Boden bedeckt ist.
Das Backrohr auf 200 Grad vorheizen.
Aus dem Teig kleine Kugeln formen, ca. 3–4 cm im Durchmesser. Die Kugeln einzeln auf dem Handteller zu Fladen drücken, Füllung in die Mitte geben und erneut zu kleinen Bällchen formen.
Die Bällchen zunächst im Margarine-Zucker-Gemisch wälzen, sodass sie rundum mit Fett bedeckt sind, und dann erst nebeneinander auf die Margarine in die Reine setzen. In ca. 30 Minuten im Rohr goldbraun backen.

Tipp Rohrnudeln schmecken auch wunderbar mit frischen Zwetschgen oder Aprikosen als Füllung. Dazu 12–14 Zwetschgen oder Aprikosen halbieren und entsteinen, dabei darauf achten, dass Sie die Früchte nicht ganz durchtrennen. 30 g Zucker und 1 TL Zimtpulver miteinander vermengen und die Obstinnenseiten großzügig damit bestreuen. Das restliche Zuckergemisch kann als Resteverwertung zur Margarine in die Bratreine wandern. Früchte anschließend wieder zusammenklappen und einzeln in die Teigbälle füllen. Weiter im Rezept wie oben verfahren.

Mix the melted margarine and sugar and pour into the roasting pan until that the bottom is completely covered.
Preheat oven to 400°F.
Form small balls of dough about 1–1 1/2 inches in diameter. Flatten each ball between the palms of your hand, place some filling in the middle, and form a small ball again. Dip the balls into the margarine-sugar mixture so that they are completely covered in fat before arranging them in rows in the baking dish, sitting in the margarine. Bake for 30 minutes until golden.

Tips & Hints Alternatively "Rohrnudeln" can also be prepared with a plum or apricot filling. Halve and pit 12–14 plums or apricots without fully severing the two halves from each other. Mix 1/8 cup sugar and 1 tsp ground cinnamon. Generously sprinkle mixture on the inside of the fruit. The left-over cinnamon sugar can be added to the margarine in the roasting pan. Close the fruit and place in balls of dough. Continue as is described above.

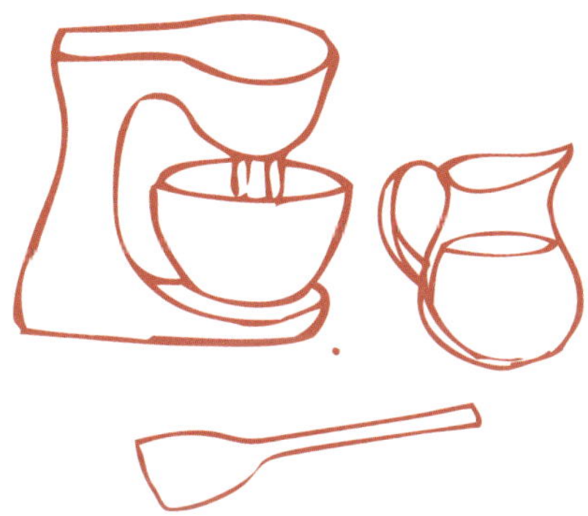

SCHEITERHAUFEN »DELUXE«

Zubereitungszeit ca. 15 Minuten + 40–45 Minuten Backzeit

Dieses Rezept ist ein klassischer »Resteverwerter«. Der traditionelle Scheiterhaufen wird mit altbackenen Semmeln oder Weißbrotscheiben zubereitet. Die »Deluxe-Version« ist meiner kreativen Chefin in dem kleinen Münchner Café, in dem ich gelegentlich arbeite, eingefallen. Immer wieder blieben uns Croissants und süße Semmeln vom Vortag über, viel zu schade, um sie wegzuschmeißen. Jetzt finden sie reißenden Absatz als edler Ofenschlupfer, wie der Scheiterhaufen in manchen Teilen Bayerns auch genannt wird.

ZUTATEN

8–10 Croissants vom Vortag – oder wahlweise 6 altbackene Semmeln
500 g tiefgefrorene Kirschen oder Himbeeren
100 g Mandelblättchen
500 ml Milch
300 g Sahne
100 g Zucker
4 Eier
1 Pck. Vanillepudding
2–3 Tropfen Vanilleextrakt – oder wahlweise Mark von 1/2 Vanilleschote

AUSSERDEM 1 kleine Auflaufform

ZUBEREITUNG

Die Croissants in dickere Scheiben schneiden und die Hälfte davon auf dem Boden der Auflaufform gleichmäßig verteilen. Die Hälfte von den tiefgefrorenen Kirschen und den Mandelblättchen auf den Croissants verteilen. Dann den Rest der Croissantscheiben drübergeben und mit Kirschen und Mandelblättchen abschließen.
Den Backofen auf 200 Grad vorheizen.
Milch, Sahne und Zucker mit den Eiern, dem Inhalt des Vanillepuddingpäckchens und dem Vanilleextrakt verrühren. Das Milch-Eier-Gemisch gleichmäßig über den Croissants verteilen. Den Scheiterhaufen ca. 40–45 Minuten im Ofen backen, bis die Flüssigkeit gestockt ist. Immer wieder mal zwischendurch den Daumentest machen, d. h. mit dem Daumen auf den Auflauf drücken. Wenn keine Flüssigkeit mehr austritt, ist der Scheiterhaufen fertig.

FRUIT CASSEROLE DELUXE

Preparation time approx. 15 minutes + 40–45 minutes baking time

This recipe is perfect for using up left overs. It is called something close to "Disaster Deluxe" in German indicating "failure" or "defeat." The traditional fruit casserole is made with old rolls or slices of white bread. The deluxe version is my employer's creation. I occasionally work at a small café in Munich and croissants and sweet rolls would be left over daily. It would have been a shame to throw them away. So my boss came up with a different version of the classic "Ofenschlupfer" (literally oven hatchling), as it is sometimes called in certain regions of Bavaria.

INGREDIENTS

8–10 day-old croissants or 6 stale bread rolls
5 cups frozen cherries or raspberries
1/2 cup almond flakes
2 cups milk
1 1/3 cups cream
1/2 cup sugar
4 eggs
1 sachet of German-style vanilla pudding powder (or ca. 1/2 cup starch mixed with pulp of 1 vanilla bean)
2–3 drops of vanilla extract or 1/2 a vanilla bean

IN ADDITION 1 casserole dish

METHOD

Cut the croissants into thick slices and evenly lay out half of them on the bottom of the dish. Spread out half of the frozen cherries and almond flakes over the layer of croissants. Now arrange the remaining croissant slices on top and evenly spread out the cherries and almond flakes on top of that layer.
Preheat oven to 400°F.
Mix the milk, cream, sugar and eggs together with the vanilla pudding powder and vanilla extract. Now evenly pour this mixture over the croissant layer. Bake for approximately 40–45 minutes until the "Scheiterhaufen" (literally "pyre" or "heap of failure") has solidified. Make sure to do the thumb test to see if it is finished. Push a small indentation on the top of the fruit casserole with your thumb. If no liquid appears any more, it has baked enough and is done.

OMAS QUARKAUFLAUF MIT BIRNEN

Zubereitungszeit ca. 20 Minuten + ca. 45–60 Minuten Backzeit

Ich kann mich noch gut daran erinnern, wie ich als kleines Mädchen aus der Schule kam, um bei meiner Oma zu Mittag zu essen. Freitags gab es immer etwas Süßes und ich dachte, dass meine Oma extra für mich diese zuckrigen Aufläufe machte, weil sie doch wusste, was ich für ein Schleckermäulchen war. Jahre später erfuhr ich, dass Oma ihres katholischen Glaubens wegen jeden Freitag auf Fleisch verzichtete – deswegen also die vielen Mehlspeisen, deren verführerische Düfte mir heute noch gegenwärtig sind.

ZUTATEN

50 g Butter, zimmerwarm
100 g Zucker
5 Eigelb
500 g Magerquark, 20% Fett i. Tr.
50 g Grieß
1 TL Backpulver
Abrieb von 1 unbehandelten Zitrone
50 g Rosinen, über Nacht in Orangensaft eingeweicht
50 g Mandelblättchen
5 Eiweiß, mit 1 Prise Salz sehr steif geschlagen
500 g Birnen, gewaschen, vom Kerngehäuse befreit und in feine Scheiben geschnitten

AUSSERDEM 1 Auflaufform, Butter zum Einfetten der Form

ZUBEREITUNG

Butter mit Zucker und Eigelben schaumig rühren. Quark unterrühren. Grieß mit Backpulver vermischen und unter die Masse rühren. Anschließend Zitronenabrieb, Rosinen (abgetropft) und Mandelblättchen beifügen. Zum Schluss den Eischnee vorsichtig unterheben.
Backofen auf 175 Grad vorheizen.
Auflaufform gut mit Butter einfetten und die Birnenscheiben als unterste Schicht auf dem Boden verteilen. Die Quarkmasse gleichmäßig über die Birnen geben und den Auflauf ca. 45 Minuten bis 1 Stunde im Ofen goldgelb backen.

GRANDMOTHER'S CURD CHEESE SOUFFLÉ RECIPE WITH PEARS

Preparation time approx. 20 minutes + approx. 45–60 minutes baking time

I can still remember as if it were just yesterday how every Friday, I would run to my grandmother's after school to have lunch. On Fridays, she would always cook or bake something sweet. For the longest time, I thought she did this because she knew I had a sweet tooth. It was only later that I discovered that she was a devout Catholic and her beliefs forbade her to eat meat on Fridays. That was the whole reason behind all those sinfully sweet dishes that I can still smell today.

INGREDIENTS

3 Tb butter at room temperature
1/2 cup sugar
3 egg yolks
2 cups low-fat curd cheese
1/2 cup semolina
1 tsp baking powder
grated lemon rind of 1 lemon
1/3 cup raisins, soaked in orange juice overnight
1/4 cup almond flakes
5 egg whites, add 1 pinch salt and beat until stiff
18 oz pears, washed, cored and sliced

IN ADDITION 1 casserole dish, butter for greasing

METHOD

Stir the butter, sugar and egg yolks until foamy. Stir in the curd cheese. Mix the semolina and baking powder and then add to the curd cheese mixture, gently stirring until all is blended together. Add the grated lemon rind, drained raisins and almond flakes. Finally, fold in the frothy egg whites.
Preheat oven to 350°F.
Generously grease the casserole dish with butter and lay out the pear slices on the bottom until it is completely covered. Evenly spread the curd cheese mixture over the layer of pears and bake for about 45–60 minutes until golden.

VEGANER REISAUFLAUF MIT SAUERKIRSCHEN UND GETROCKNETEN APRIKOSEN

Zubereitungszeit ca. 15 Minuten + Garzeit ca. 120 Minuten

Als ich noch ein kleines Mädchen war, gab es bei meiner Großmutter fast jeden Freitag einen süßen Auflauf zum Mittagessen. Nicht selten kam dabei, neben dem Quarkauflauf von Seite 25, ein leckerer Reisauflauf mit Sauerkirschen auf den Tisch.

Das folgende Rezept wurde von mir etwas »modernisiert« und abgewandelt, sodass anstatt normaler Milch und Sahne Sojaprodukte zum Einsatz kommen; sie geben dem Auflauf einen nussigen Geschmack. Sie können aber natürlich auch, wie ursprünglich im Rezept meiner Oma, auf ganz normale Vollmilch und süßen Rahm zurückgreifen – ganz nach Gusto.

ZUTATEN

250 g Rundkornreis, bevorzugt zum Zubereiten von Milchreis, oder Risottoreis
ca. 150 g Rohrohrzucker
ca. 750 ml Sojamilch
100 g Sojasahne
1 Msp. Muskat
1 großes Glas Sauerkirschen, abgetropft
ca. 150 g getrocknete, ungeschwefelte Aprikosen, in feine Scheibchen geschnitten

AUSSERDEM etwas Sonnenblumenöl zum Einfetten der Form, 1–2 TL Zimtpulver zum Bestreuen des fertigen Auflaufs

ZUBEREITUNG

Den Backofen auf 150 Grad vorheizen.

Den Reis zunächst waschen und abtropfen lassen, dann in der eingefetteten Form gleichmäßig verteilen. Den Zucker mit Milch und Sahne gut verrühren, das Ganze mit Muskat würzen und anschließend über den Reis gießen. Sauerkirschen und Aprikosen untermischen und die Form in den vorgeheizten Ofen schieben.

Rühren Sie während der Garzeit immer wieder um, damit sich auf dem Reisauflauf keine dunkle Haut bildet. Servieren Sie ihn dann lauwarm und mit etwas Zimt bestreut.

VEGAN RICE CAKE WITH SOUR CHERRIES AND DRIED APRICOTS

Preparation time approx. 15 minutes + cooking time approx. 120 minutes

When I was a child, my grandmother made a sweet dish for lunch almost every Friday. Every once in a while she made a delicious rice cake with sour cherries as a variation to the curd cheese soufflé.

The following recipe has been “modernized” and modified by me so that the milk and cream are substituted with soy products, adding a wonderfully nutty flavor. However, you can, of course, use whole milk and cream in this recipe, just as my grandmother did back then.

INGREDIENTS

1 cup round grain rice (the kind used for rice pudding) or risotto rice
approx. 2/3 cup raw cane sugar
approx. 3 cups soy milk
scant 1/2 cup soy whip
just a trace of nutmeg
1 large glass drained sour cherries
approx. 1 cup dried unsulfured apricots, finely sliced

IN ADDITION some sunflower oil for greasing, 1–2 tsp ground cinnamon for dusting

METHOD

Preheat oven to 300°F.

After the rice is washed and drained, evenly spread it out on the bottom of the greased casserole dish. Thoroughly blend the milk and cream together adding a hint of nutmeg. Pour over the rice. Now stir in the sour cherries and dried apricots and place in the preheated oven.

Stir constantly while cooking so that no dark skin on the rice pudding forms (especially if you have used soy milk). Only towards the end, during the last 20 minutes, a nice golden crust should form. Serve it lukewarm and sprinkled with some cinnamon.

Schmarrnvariationen

Variations on Scrambled Pancakes

Bei Kaiserschmarrn und Co. denken viele sofort an zünftige Hüttenabende in den Bergen, redlich verdient nach einem langen Anstieg oder nach einem Tag auf der Skipiste. Aber auch drunten im Tal hat der Schmarrn seinen festen Platz auf den regionalen Speisekarten.

When it comes to "Kaiserschmarrn" and Co, cozy cabin evenings in the mountains with lots of rich, hearty food come to mind, well-earned after a long hike or after a day on the slopes. But also down in the valley, the "Kaiserschmarrn" has its deserved spot on the regional menus.

APFEL-NUSS-SCHMARRN

Zubereitungszeit ca. 30 Minuten

ZUTATEN

FÜR DEN TEIG

375 g Mehl
500 ml kalte Milch
1 Prise Salz
4 Eier
3 EL Butterschmalz oder Margarine
3 säuerliche Äpfel, geschält, vom Kerngehäuse befreit, geviertelt und in dünne Scheiben geschnitten
100 g gehackte Nüsse, z. B. Haselnüsse oder Mandeln

AUSSERDEM 1 große, beschichtete Pfanne mit Deckel, Zimt-Zucker-Gemisch

ZUBEREITUNG

Mehl in eine Schüssel geben. Milch, Salz und Eier zugeben und miteinander verrühren, sodass ein glatter, zäher Teig entsteht, der etwas dicker als normaler Pfannkuchenteig sein sollte. Teig beiseite stellen.
Butterschmalz oder Margarine in die Pfanne geben und erhitzen. Äpfel und Nüsse zugeben und unter ständigem Rühren rösten; die Äpfel sollten leicht weich werden. Nun den Teig zu den Äpfeln und Nüssen in die Pfanne füllen und umrühren, damit sich alles gut miteinander vermischt.
Wie bei einem klassischen Omelette bei geschlossenem Deckel die Unterseite goldgelb backen. Dann das Ganze wenden und die andere Seite – nun bei offenem Deckel! – ebenfalls goldgelb backen.
Anschließend alles in der Pfanne in kleine Stücke stechen oder reißen und goldbraun ausbacken. Falls nötig, noch etwas Fett zugeben. Noch heiß mit Zimt und Zucker bestreuen.

APPLE NUT PANCAKE

Preparation time approx. 30 minutes

INGREDIENTS

FOR THE DOUGH

3 cups flour
2 cups cold milk
1 pinch salt
4 eggs
5 Tb clarified butter or margarine
3 tart apples, peeled, cored, quartered and thinly sliced
1 cup chopped nuts, such as hazelnuts or almonds

IN ADDITION 1 large, coated pan with lid, cinnamon-sugar mixture

METHOD

Put flour in a bowl. Mix milk, salt and eggs with each other to a smooth, tough dough, which should be slightly thicker than normal pancake batter. Then put the dough aside.
Heat clarified butter or margarine in the pan. Add apples and nuts and roast, stirring; the apples should be slightly soft. Now add the dough to the apples and nuts into the pan and stir so that everything is well mixed.
Bake as a classic omelette, with the lid closed, till golden on the bottom. Then turn the whole thing and bake the other side – this time with the lid open – also till golden brown.
Then tear or cut everything in the pan into small pieces and continue roasting till it is all nicely darkly golden brown. If needed, add some fat. While still hot, sprinkle with cinnamon and sugar.

Tipps

* Servieren Sie dazu selbst gemachten Eierlikör (s. S. 116), den Sie zusätzlich über den heißen Schmarrn träufeln oder im Schnapsglas separat reichen.
* Sie können die Nüsse auch durch Rosinen ersetzen. Besonders fein schmeckt es, wenn Sie die Rosinen vorher 30 Minuten in Hochprozentigem, z. B. Weinbrand, einlegen.
* Die Äpfel lassen sich auch durch entsteinte und geviertelte Zwetschgen ersetzen, deren Saft dem Schmarrn eine wunderbare Karamellnote verleiht.

Tips and Hints

* Serve with homemade eggnog (see pg. 116), which can also be drizzled over onto the hot pancakes or offered separately in a shot glass.
* You can replace the nuts with raisins. It tastes even lusher when the raisins are soaked beforehand in hard liquor, such as brandy, for about 30 minutes.
* Apples can be replaced by quartered and pitted plums, whose juice adds a wonderful caramel note.

GRIESSSCHMARRN MIT RHABARBERKOMPOTT

Zubereitungszeit inkl. Abkühlzeiten für Kompott und Grieß ca. 1 Stunde 20 Minuten

Dieses Rezept ist uralt. Ich habe es im Nachlass einer hochbetagten Bäuerin gefunden – die alte deutsche Handschrift, in engen, verblichenen Lettern und mit Bleistift geschrieben, konnte ich zunächst kaum entziffern. Grießschmarrn kam, wie auch der Mehlschmarrn – eine dickere Form des herkömmlichen Pfannenkuchenteigs –, in früheren Zeiten recht oft auf den bäuerlichen Tisch. Er verlangte keinen großen Aufwand und machte die Mägen satt und zufrieden, sodass nach dem Essen wieder alle an ihr hartes Tagwerk gehen konnten. Ursprünglich aß man den Schmarrn pur oder mit etwas Kompott, wie im nachstehenden Rezept. Zucker war zu kostbar. Aber Sie können Ihren Grießschmarrn natürlich auch mit Zimt und Zucker verfeinern.

ZUTATEN

FÜR DAS KOMPOTT

1 kg Rhabarber, gewaschen und in kleine Stücke geschnitten
150 g Zucker
evtl. 1 EL Vanillezucker
Abrieb von 1/2 unbehandelten Zitrone oder Orange

FÜR DEN SCHMARRN

500 ml Vollmilch
250 g Weizengrieß
5 Eier
1 Prise Salz

AUSSERDEM 1–2 EL Butterschmalz zum Ausbacken des Schmarrns, 1 große beschichtete Pfanne

ZUBEREITUNG

Zunächst die Rhabarberstücke für das Kompott in einen Topf geben und mit dem Zucker vermengen. Beiseitestellen und ca. 1 Stunde ziehen lassen. Gelegentlich umrühren.
Dann Topf samt Rhabarberstücken auf den Herd stellen und Zitronen- oder Orangenabrieb zugeben. Ohne Zugabe von Wasser erhitzen und bei schwacher Hitze köcheln lassen, bis

SEMOLINA PANCAKE WITH RHUBARB COMPOTE

Preparation time including cooling periods for compote and semolina approx. 1 hour 20 minutes

This recipe is very old. I found it on an elderly farmer's wife estate in tightly bound, faded letters, written in pencil in the old German handwriting, which at first I could barely decipher. In the past, semolina pancakes, as were also flour pancakes – a thicker version of the traditional pancake – were quite often present on the farm table. It demanded no effort to make and yet sated and satisfied so that after dinner all could return to their hard daily chores. Originally, the pancakes were eaten alone or with some compote, as in the following recipe. Sugar was too precious. But, of course, you can refine your semolina pancakes with cinnamon and sugar.

INGREDIENTS

FOR THE COMPOTE

35 oz rhubarb, washed and cut into small pieces
2/3 cup sugar
may 1 Tb vanilla sugar
rind of 1/2 of an untreated lemon or orange

FOR THE PANCAKE

2 cups whole milk
1 1/2 cups semolina
5 eggs
1 pinch salt

IN ADDITION 2–3 1/2 Tb clarified butter for frying the "Schmarrns" (the cut up pancakes), 1 large nonstick skillet

METHOD

Start by placing the rhubarb pieces in a pot and mix with the sugar to stew. Set aside for about 1 hour. Stirring occasionally.
Then place the pot along with rhubarb pieces on the stove and add the grated lemon or orange rind. Let it simmer on low heat until the rhubarb is soft without adding any water. Stirring occasionally. Remove from heat and allow to cool. Possibly add some sugar to sweeten.
While the rhubarb is simmering, bring the milk to a boil in another pan and stir in the semolina. Cook while stirring, until

der Rhabarber weich ist. Gelegentlich umrühren. Vom Herd nehmen und auskühlen lassen. Eventuell nachsüßen.
Während der Rhabarber köchelt, in einem anderen Topf die Milch zum Kochen bringen und den Grieß einrühren. Unter ständigem Rühren garen, bis ein sämiger Brei entsteht. Vom Herd nehmen und komplett auskühlen lassen.
Dann die Eier nach und nach unter den Grießbrei rühren und zum Schluss Salz zugeben.
Butterschmalz in einer Pfanne erhitzen und die Grießmasse hineingeben. Auf der unteren Seite goldgelb backen. Wenden und mit der anderen Seite ebenso verfahren. Dann in Stücke reißen oder schneiden und unter Rühren goldbraun fertig backen – eventuell noch etwas Butterschmalz zugeben.

a creamy paste is formed. Remove from heat and allow to cool completely.
Then gradually stir the eggs into the semolina and finally add a pinch of salt.
Heat clarified butter in a pan and add the semolina mixture. Bake until golden on the bottom. Turn and proceed as with the other side. Then tear or cut into pieces and finish baking until golden brown, stirring all the while – possibly adding some more clarified butter.

KAISERSCHMARRN

Für 2 hungrige Personen als Hauptmahlzeit oder für 4 Leute zum Dessert
Zubereitungszeit inkl. Zeit zum Quellen für den Teig ca. 45 Minuten

ZUTATEN

200 g Mehl
400 ml kalte Milch
4 Eigelb
2 EL zerlassene Butter
2 EL Zucker
1 Prise Salz
4 Eiweiß

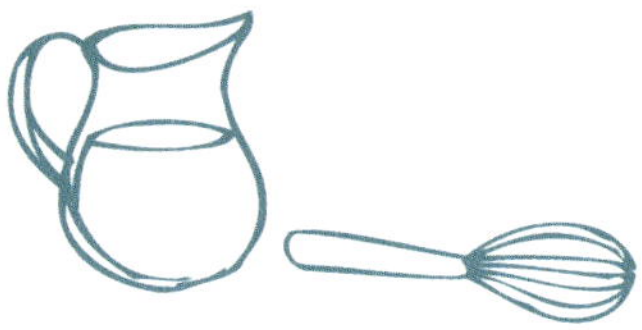

AUSSERDEM 2–3 EL Butterschmalz oder Margarine zum Ausbacken, 1 große beschichtete Pfanne mit Deckel, Puderzucker oder Zimt-Zucker-Gemisch

ZUBEREITUNG

Mehl, Milch, Eigelbe, zerlassene Butter, 1 EL Zucker und 1 Prise Salz in eine Schüssel geben und zu einem glatten, zähen Teig verrühren. Zugedeckt ca. 30 Minuten quellen lassen.
Anschließend Eiweiße mit 1 EL Zucker steif schlagen und sacht unter den Teig heben.
Butterschmalz oder Margarine in der Pfanne erhitzen, den Teig einfüllen und bei geschlossenem Deckel backen. Wenn die Unterseite eine goldgelbe Farbe angenommen hat, den Teig wenden und die zweite Seite ohne Deckel ebenfalls goldgelb backen. Anschließend den Kaiserschmarrn in der Pfanne in Stücke stechen oder reißen und goldbraun fertig backen. Noch warm mit Puderzucker oder Zimt und Zucker bestreuen.

Tipps

* *Sehr lecker schmeckt der Kaiserschmarrn, wenn Sie den Puderzucker in der Pfanne mitkaramellisieren, anstatt ihn am Ende über den Schmarrn zu stäuben. Dazu machen Sie in der Pfanne mit dem Kaiserschmarrn ein Eckchen frei und stäuben 1–2 TL Puderzucker hinein. Ist der Puderzucker karamellisiert – das geht sehr schnell! –, geben Sie den Kaiserschmarrn zurück und vermengen das Ganze.*
* *Zum Kaiserschmarrn reicht man traditionell Apfelmus.*

EMPEROR'S CUTUPS

("KAISERSCHMARRN")

Recipe is for 2 hungry people as a main dish or for 4 people for dessert
Preparation time including time for the dough to set approx. 45 minutes

INGREDIENTS

1 3/5 cups flour
1 3/4 cups cold milk
4 egg yolks
2 Tb melted butter
2 Tb sugar
1 pinch salt
4 egg whites

IN ADDITION 3 1/2–5 Tb clarified butter or margarine for frying, 1 large nonstick skillet with lid, powdered sugar or cinnamon-sugar mixture

METHOD

Add flour, milk, egg yolks, melted butter, 1 Tb sugar and 1 pinch of salt in a bowl and mix to a smooth, chewy dough. Allow to set and swell 30 minutes.
Then beat egg whites with 1 Tb sugar until stiff and gently fold in the mixture.
Add clarified butter or margarine to a pan heat, pour the dough and bake with the lid closed. Once the bottom has a golden color, turn the dough and bake the other side without a cover also until golden brown. Then tear or cut the "Kaiserschmarrn" in the pan into pieces and bake until golden brown. While still hot sprinkle with powdered sugar or cinnamon sugar.

Tips and Hints

* *The Kaiserschmarrn tastes even tastier if you caramelize the powdered sugar in the pan rather than just dust it at the end. Clear a corner in the pan with the Kaiserschmarrn and dust 1–2 tsp powdered sugar into it. Powdered sugar caramelizes very fast! Then return the Kaiserschmarrn to this corner and mix the whole thing.*
* *Kaiserschmarrn is traditionally served with apple sauce.*

Strudel

Strudel Variations

APFELSTRUDEL

Zubereitungszeit 45 Minuten inkl. 20 Minuten Ruhezeit für den Teig + Backzeit ca. 30 Minuten

Der Apfelstrudel ist aus der bayerischen Küche nicht mehr wegzudenken. Dabei ist er eigentlich ein waschechter Österreicher und reiht sich nahtlos unter so berühmte k. u. k. (königlich-kaiserliche) Mehlspeisen wie den Marillenknödeln, den Salzburger Nockerl und dem klassischen Kaiserschmarrn (s. S. 32) ein.

ZUTATEN

FÜR DEN TEIG

200 g Mehl
1 Ei
1 TL Apfelessig
1 Prise Salz
2 EL zerlassene Butter
ca. 50 ml warmes Wasser

FÜR DIE FÜLLUNG

80 g Butter
80–100 g Semmelbrösel
4 große säuerliche Äpfel, geschält, entkernt, geviertelt und in ca. 3 mm dicke Scheiben geschnitten
150 g Zucker
1 TL Zimt
2 EL Rum oder Weinbrand
2 TL (1 Pck.) Vanillezucker
nach Belieben 80 g Rosinen

AUSSERDEM etwas Mehl zum Bestäuben, 2 EL neutrales Öl und 100 g zerlassene Butter zum Bestreichen des fertigen Teigs, 1 sauberes, gemustertes Geschirrtuch, Backblech, Backpapier, Puderzucker zum Bestäuben

ZUBEREITUNG

Die Zutaten für den Strudelteig in eine Schüssel geben und zu einem festen, glatten Teig verarbeiten. Die Teigkugel auf ein bemehltes Arbeitsbrett legen und mit Öl bestreichen. Eine Schüssel mit heißem Wasser ausschwenken und den Teig mit der Schüssel abdecken. 20 Minuten ruhen lassen.
Währenddessen Butter für die Füllung in einer Pfanne erhitzen und die Semmelbrösel darin goldgelb anrösten. Beiseitestellen. Die restlichen Zutaten für die Strudelfüllung – mit oder ohne

APPLE STRUDEL

Preparation time 45 minutes including 20 minutes resting time for the dough + baking time 30 minutes

The Apple strudel is indispensable for Bavarian cuisine. Yet it is actually a genuine Austrian dish and joins seamlessly in such famous royal and imperial pastries as the "Marillenknödel" (Apricot dumplings), the Salzburg dumplings and the traditional Kaiserschmarrn (see pg. 32).

INGREDIENTS

FOR THE DOUGH

1 3/5 cups flour
1 egg
1 tsp apple vinegar
1 pinch salt
2 Tb melted butter
approx. 1/4 cup warm water

FOR THE FILLING

5 1/2 Tb butter
6 Tb breadcrumbs
4 large tart apples, peeled, cored, quartered and cut into slices about 1/10 inch thickness
2/3 cup sugar
1 tsp cinnamon
2 Tb rum or brandy
2 tsp (1 sachet) vanilla sugar
1/2 cup raisins to taste

IN ADDITION flour for dusting, 2 Tb neutral oil and 7 Tb melted butter to coat the finished dough, 1 clean, patterned dishcloth, baking sheet, baking paper, powdered sugar for dusting

METHOD

Combine the ingredients for the strudel dough in a bowl and process to a smooth, firm dough. Place the ball of dough on a floured work surface and brush with oil. Flush a bowl with hot water, place dough in the bowl and cover. Let rest for 20 minutes.
Meanwhile heat butter for the filling in a pan and sauté the breadcrumbs until golden. Set aside. Combine the remaining ingredients for the strudel filling – with or without raisins, according to taste – in a bowl and mix well.

Rosinen, ganz nach Geschmack – in eine Schüssel geben und gut vermengen.
Den Backofen auf 200 Grad vorheizen. Das gemusterte Geschirrtuch leicht mit Mehl bestäuben und den Teig darauf hauchdünn ausrollen. Zum Abschluss mit den Fingern vorsichtig auseinanderziehen, bis das Muster des Küchentuchs durchscheint.
Den Strudelteig mit zerlassener Butter bestreichen und mit den Semmelbröseln bestreuen. Dann die Äpfel auf dem oberen oder dem unteren Teigdrittel gleichmäßig verteilen. Das Küchentuch anheben und den Strudel von der belegten Seite aus einrollen. Den Strudel auf ein mit Backpapier ausgelegtes Backblech legen und mit zerlassener Butter bestreichen. Ca. 30 Minuten im Ofen backen. Zum Servieren mit Puderzucker bestäuben.

Tipp Sie können Ihren Strudel auch mit süßer und saurer Sahne aufpeppen – so wird aus einem schlichten Apfelstrudel ein leckerer Apfel-Rahm-Strudel. Dazu zuerst 200 g saure Sahne auf den Strudelteig streichen, dann weiter mit den Semmelbröseln und der Apfelfüllung wie oben verfahren. Den Strudel im Ofen ca. 20 Minuten vorbacken. Anschließend 200 g süße Sahne über dem Strudel verteilen, das Ganze mit Alufolie abdecken und den Strudel fertig backen, bis die Sahne gestockt ist.

Preheat the oven to 400°F.
Dust the patterned dishcloth lightly with flour and roll out the dough paper thin on it. At the end gently pull it apart with your fingers until it is so thin that the pattern of the kitchen cloth is visible.
Brush the strudel dough with melted butter and sprinkle with the bread crumbs. Then distribute the apples on the top or the bottom third of the dough evenly. Lift the towel and roll the strudel from the filled side. Place the strudel on a baking sheet lined with parchment paper and brush with melted butter. Bake about 30 minutes in the oven. Serve sprinkled with powdered sugar.

Tips and Hints You can spice up your strudel with sweet and sour cream – and turn a simple apple strudel into a delicious apple cream pie. First spread 1 cup sour cream on the strudel dough, then continue with the breadcrumbs and the apple filling as above. Preback the strudel in the oven for 20 minutes. Then spread 1 cup sweet cream all over the strudel and cover with tinfoil cover, place in the oven and bake the strudel until the cream thickens.

LEBKUCHENSTRUDEL

Zubereitungszeit ca. 1 Stunde inkl. 20 Minuten Ruhezeit für Füllung und Teig + Backzeit ca. 35 Minuten

Der Lebkuchenstrudel ist ein toller Resteverwerter für altbackene Lebkuchen – und ein leckerer obendrein. Genau genommen fällt dieser Strudel ja unter die Rubrik »Weihnachten«, aber er schmeckt auch im Januar und Februar ziemlich gut. Ein echter Winterklassiker eben!

ZUTATEN

FÜR DEN TEIG

200 g Mehl
1 Ei
1 TL Apfelessig
2 EL zerlassene Butter
50 ml warmes Wasser
2 EL zerlassene Butter zum Bestreichen des Teigs

FÜR DIE FÜLLUNG

300 g altbackene oder frische Lebkuchen, in kleine Würfel geschnitten
2 säuerliche Äpfel, geschält, vom Kerngehäuse befreit und klein gewürfelt
150 g Sauerrahm
ca. 50 ml Milch
2 EL Rosinen
2 EL Mandelblättchen
2 TL (1 Pck.) Vanillezucker
1–2 EL Rum
genügend zerlassene Butter zum Bestreichen der Teiginnen- und der Strudeloberfläche

AUSSERDEM 1 Geschirrtuch mit Muster, Backblech, Backpapier

ZUBEREITUNG

Aus den Zutaten für den Teig einen festen, glatten Teig kneten. Die Oberfläche der Teigkugel mit zerlassener Butter bepinseln. Eine Schüssel mit heißem Wasser ausschwenken und den Teig damit abdecken. Mindestens 20 Minuten ruhen lassen.
Währenddessen die Füllung vorbereiten. Dazu die Lebkuchenwürfel zusammen mit den Äpfeln, dem Sauerrahm, der Milch und den Rosinen in eine Schüssel geben und gut vermengen. Ebenfalls ca. 20 Minuten zum Quellen beiseitestellen. Danach Mandeln, Vanillezucker und Rum unter die Masse rühren.

GINGERBREAD STRUDEL

Preparation time approx. 1 hour including 20 minutes resting time + approx. 35 minutes baking time

Gingerbread strudel is a lovely – and on top of it delicious – way to recycle gingerbread leftovers. Actually, gingerbread traditionally belongs to the Christmas dessert category, but it tastes just as good in January and February. A wonderful winter treat for everyone.

INGREDIENTS

FOR THE DOUGH

1 3/5 cups flour
1 egg
1 tsp apple vinegar
2 Tb melted butter
approx. 1/4 cup warm water
2 Tb melted butter for brushing the dough

FOR THE FILLING

stale or fresh gingerbread, cut into small cubes
2 tart apples, peeled, cored and cut into small cubes
3/4 cup sour cream
approx. 1/4 cup milk
2 Tb raisins
2 Tb almond flakes
2 tsp (1 sachet) vanilla sugar
1–2 Tb rum
plenty of melted butter for brushing the dough

IN ADDITION 1 patterned kitchen towel, baking sheet, baking parchment

METHOD

Knead together the ingredients for the dough until they have been worked into a smooth, firm mixture. Brush the ball of dough with melted butter. Rinse out a bowl with hot water and place over the dough; let it rest for 20 minutes.
Meanwhile prepare the filling. Place the apples, sour cream, milk and raisins in a bowl and blend thoroughly; set aside for 20 minutes. Then stir in the almond flakes, vanilla sugar and rum.
Preheat oven to 350°F.
Dust the patterned kitchen towel with flour and roll out the dough until paper-thin. Using your fingers, carefully spread the dough until the pattern on the kitchen towel shows through.

Backrohr auf 180 Grad vorheizen.
Das Geschirrtuch leicht mit Mehl bestäuben und den Strudelteig darauf ausrollen; zum Schluss mit den Händen fein auseinanderziehen, sodass das Muster durch die Teigmembran gut zu erkennen ist. Die Teigfläche mit zerlassener Butter einstreichen. Die Lebkuchenfüllung auf den unteren zwei Dritteln gleichmäßig verteilen und dann den Strudel vorsichtig aufrollen. Auf dem mit Backpapier belegten Backblech platzieren und die Oberfläche ebenfalls mit zerlassener Butter bestreichen. Im Ofen ca. 35 Minuten goldbraun backen.

Then brush the dough with melted butter. Spread the gingerbread filling onto either the upper or lower third of the dough. Lift the filling-end of the kitchen towel and roll into a strudel shape. Place the strudel on a baking sheet lined with baking parchment and brush again with melted butter; bake for about 35 minutes until golden.

TOPFENSTRUDEL

Zubereitungszeit ca. 40 Minuten + ca. 1 Stunde Backzeit

ZUTATEN

FÜR DEN TEIG

200 g Mehl
1 Ei
1 TL Obstessig
1 Prise Salz
2 EL zerlassene Butter
50 ml warmes Wasser
2 EL Sonnenblumenöl

FÜR DIE FÜLLUNG

50 g Rosinen
50 g Sultaninen
75 g Butter, zimmerwarm
2 Eier
500 g Topfen (Magerquark), 20% Fett i. Tr.
80 g Zucker
100 g Sahne
100 g saure Sahne

AUSSERDEM gemustertes Geschirrtuch, etwas Mehl, 100 g zerlassene Butter zum Bestreichen des Strudelteigs, Alufolie, Backpapier, Backblech, Puderzucker zum Bestäuben

ZUBEREITUNG

Alle Zutaten für den Teig, mit Ausnahme des Sonnenblumenöls, zu einem glatten Teig verkneten. Anschließend die Oberfläche des Teigballs mit Sonnenblumenöl bestreichen und 20 Minuten lang unter einer mit heißem Wasser ausgeschwenkten Schüssel ruhen lassen.
Währenddessen Rosinen und Sultaninen in einer Schüssel mit heißem Wasser waschen und dann abtropfen lassen. Butter schaumig schlagen. Eier und die restlichen Zutaten für die Füllung zugeben und vermengen. Rosinen und Sultaninen unterheben.
Den Backofen auf 200 Grad vorheizen.
Den Teig auf dem bemehlten Geschirrtuch ausrollen und zum Schluss mit den Händen hauchdünn ausziehen, sodass das Muster des Küchentuchs durch den Strudelteig durchscheint.
Den Strudelteig mit zerlassener Butter einpinseln und die Füllung gleichmäßig darauf verteilen. An den Rändern einschlagen. Das Küchentuch anheben und den Strudel

CURD CHEESE STRUDEL

Preparation time approx. 40 minutes + approx. 1 hour baking time

INGREDIENTS

FOR THE DOUGH

1 3/5 cups flour
1 egg
1 tsp apple vinegar
1 pinch salt
2 Tb melted butter
scant 1/4 cup warm water
2 Tb sunflower oil

FOR THE FILLING

1/3 cup raisins
scant 1/3 cup sultanas
5 Tb butter at room temperature
2 eggs
2 cups low-fat curd cheese
1/3 cup sugar
scant 1/2 cup cream
scant 1/2 cup sour cream

IN ADDITION patterned kitchen towel, flour, 7 Tb melted butter for brushing the dough, aluminum foil, backing parchment, backing sheet, powdered sugar for dusting

METHOD

Mix all ingredients for the dough, except the sunflower oil, together and knead until dough is smooth. Brush the ball of dough with the sunflower oil. Rinse out a bowl with hot water and invert it over the dough and let it rest for 20 minutes.
Meanwhile, rinse the raisins with hot water and let drain.
Cream the butter. Add the eggs and the remaining ingredients for the filling and mix. Fold in the two different types of raisins.
Preheat oven to 400°F.
Place the dough on a floured kitchen towel with a pattern; roll out into a rectangle and finish using your hands pat out the dough paper-thin. It should be thin enough for the pattern on the kitchen towel to show through.
Brush the strudel dough with the melted butter and evenly spread the filling over it. Turn up the edges. Lift the end of the kitchen towel and carefully roll the strudel. Slide the strudel

vorsichtig einrollen. Den Strudel auf ein mit Backpapier ausgelegtes Backblech gleiten lassen. Da der Topfenstrudel grundsätzlich dazu neigt, im Backrohr auseinanderzufließen, stützt man den Strudel links und rechts mit Wülsten aus Alufolie ab oder man legt ihn in eine extra dafür konzipierte Strudelform.
Den Topfenstrudel ca. 1 Stunde im Rohr backen, anschließend abkühlen lassen und mit Puderzucker bestäuben.

onto a baking sheet lined with baking parchment and place in the oven.
Since the filling in a curd cheese strudel tends to run during baking, prop it up on both sides with rolls of aluminum foil or use a baking pan made especially for this type of strudel.
Bake for about 1 hour. Remove from oven, let it cool completely and then sprinkle with powdered sugar.

KIRSCHSTRUDEL

Zubereitungszeit inkl. Ruhe- und Auskühlzeiten 50 Minuten + ca. 40 Minuten Backzeit

ZUTATEN

FÜR DIE FÜLLUNG

750 g tiefgefrorene Sauerkirschen
80 g Zucker
1–2 EL Kirschwasser
1 Vanilleschote, mit einem scharfen Messer eingeritzt
2 EL Speisestärke
4 EL Wasser
80 g Butter
100 g Semmelbrösel
50 g gemahlene Mandeln

FÜR DEN TEIG

200 g Mehl
1 Ei
1 TL Apfelessig
2 EL zerlassene Butter
50 ml warmes Wasser
2 EL Sonnenblumenöl zum Bestreichen der Teiginnenfläche

AUSSERDEM gemustertes Geschirrtuch, etwas Mehl, 100 g zerlassene Butter zum Bestreichen des Strudelteigs, Alufolie, Backpapier, Backblech

ZUBEREITUNG

Zuerst die Füllung vorbereiten: Die gefrorenen Kirschen mit Zucker, Kirschwasser und Vanilleschote in einen Topf geben und bei schwacher Hitze aufkochen lassen. Stärke und Wasser glatt miteinander verrühren und unter die Kirschen rühren. Ca. 1 Minute köcheln lassen, dann vom Herd nehmen und 30 Minuten auskühlen lassen. Vanilleschote entfernen.
Butter in einer Pfanne erhitzen und leicht braun werden lassen. Semmelbrösel und Mandeln zugeben und goldgelb anrösten. Beiseitestellen und auskühlen lassen.
Währenddessen die Zutaten für den Strudelteig, mit Ausnahme des Sonnenblumenöls, zu einem glatten Teig verkneten. Die Oberfläche der Teigkugel mit Sonnenblumenöl einpinseln. Eine Schüssel mit heißem Wasser ausschwenken und den Teig mit der Schüssel abdecken. 20 Minuten ruhen lassen.
Anschließend den Backofen auf 200 Grad vorheizen.

CHERRY STRUDEL

Preparation time 50 minutes including resting and cooling time + approx. 40 minutes baking time

INGREDIENTS

FOR THE FILLING

27 oz frozen sour cherries
1/3 cup sugar
1–2 Tb cherry brandy (Kirschwasser)
1 carved vanilla bean
2 Tb starch
4 Tb water
5 1/2 Tb butter
6 Tb dried breadcrumbs
1/2 cup ground almonds

FOR THE DOUGH

1 3/5 cups flour
1 egg
1 tsp apple vinegar
2 Tb melted butter
approx. 1/4 cup warm water
2 Tb sunflower oil for brushing the inside of the dough

IN ADDITION patterned kitchen towel, some flour, 7 Tb melted butter for brushing the dough, aluminum foil, baking parchment, baking sheet

METHOD

First prepare the filling; place the frozen cherries, sugar, Kirschwasser and the carved vanilla bean in a pot and slowly bring to the boil. Then mix the starch and water until completely blended, then stir into the cherries. Let simmer for one minute. Remove from heat and let it cool for about 30 minutes. Remove the vanilla bean. Melt some butter in a saucepan and let it brown before adding the breadcrumbs and almond flakes. Roast these until golden, then set aside and let cool. Meanwhile knead together all ingredients for the dough – except the sunflower oil – until smooth. Brush the ball of dough with the sunflower oil. Rinse out a bowl with hot water and place over the dough; let rest for 20 minutes.
Preheat oven to 400°F.
Dust the patterned kitchen towel with flour and roll out the dough until paper-thin. Using your fingers, carefully spread the dough until the pattern on the kitchen towel shows through.

Ein gemustertes Geschirrtuch leicht mit Mehl bestäuben und den Teig darauf ausrollen. Zum Abschluss mit den Fingern vorsichtig auseinanderziehen, bis das Muster des Küchentuchs durchscheint. Den Strudelteig mit etwas zerlassener Butter bestreichen und mit dem Semmelbrösel-Mandel-Gemisch bestreuen. Kirschen auf der Längsseite des Teigs bis leicht über die Mitte hin gleichmäßig verteilen, dabei einen schmalen, äußeren Rand von ca. 2 cm frei lassen. Die Kirschen leicht flach drücken, dann die seitlichen Teigränder nach innen einschlagen. Das Küchentuch anheben und von der belegten Seite aus den Strudel einrollen. Den Strudel mit dem Rest der zerlassenen Butter einpinseln und auf ein mit Backpapier ausgelegtes Backblech legen. Wülste aus Alufolie stützen den Strudel auf beiden Seiten ab, sodass er beim Backen nicht außer Form gerät.
Ca. 40 Minuten im Ofen backen. Falls Sie merken, dass die Oberfläche des Strudels während des Backens zu trocken wird, gegebenenfalls nochmals mit zerlassener Butter einpinseln. Vor dem Anschneiden und Servieren ca. 15 Minuten auskühlen lassen.

Tipp Zu Kirschstrudel passt besonders gut Vanilleeis.

Then brush the dough with melted butter. Sprinkle with the almond-breadcrumb mix. Leaving an inch gap, evenly spread the cherry filling from the longer side up to an imaginary middle line of the rectangular dough. Gently flatten the cherries and then fold in the edges. Lift the filling-end of the kitchen towel and roll into a strudel shape. Place the strudel on a baking sheet lined with baking parchment and brush again with melted butter; to stabilize the strudel and to make sure it keeps its shape, place two thick aluminum logs (made of crumbled foil) on either side of the strudel. Bake for about 40 minutes until golden. If you notice the strudel is drying out during baking, brush again with the melted butter. Let cool for about 15 minutes before serving.

Tips & Hints Vanilla ice cream goes especially well with cherry strudel.

Schmalzgebäck

Deep-fried Pastries

Schmalzgebäck hat in Bayern seinen festen Platz im kirchlichen Jahreslauf. So werden z. B. heute noch landauf, landab in vielen Bäckereien zur traditionellen Kirchweih im Oktober Kirchweihnudeln angeboten. Und zum Erntedankfest, das Anfang Oktober in den Gotteshäusern feierlich begangen wird, hat die Auszogene ihren großen Auftritt.
In früheren Zeiten schickte die Bäuerin ihren Männern oft Schmalzgebäck aufs Feld hinaus, damit sie bei Kräften blieben, und mittags kamen nicht selten diverse Schmalznudeln anstatt von Brot als Beilage zur Suppe auf den Tisch. Heutzutage hat die gemeine Nudel ihren angestammten Platz auf vielen nachmittäglichen Kaffeetafeln gefunden. Schmalzgebäck lässt sich übrigens problemlos einfrieren. Bei Bedarf einfach portionsweise sanft im Backofen (60–80 Grad) oder in der Mikrowelle auftauen und aufwärmen.

Church-oriented holidays and deep-fried pastries belong together in Bavaria. This is why all over the state bakeries will sell "Kirchweihnudeln" (literally: parish festival noodles) only in October during the parish festival period. During the beginning of October, when all God-fearing households celebrate Thanksgiving, you will find "Auszogene" (pulled pastry) everywhere.
Back in the old days, the farmers' wives would pack fried pastries for their husbands' snacks to keep them energized throughout the day for their hard labor. For lunch it was also not unusual for deep-fried pastries to be served as a side to soup instead of bread. Nowadays it is a common afternoon coffee dish.
By the way, these types of pastries are ideal for freezing. Whenever some is needed, just cut off a portion and slowly thaw in an oven (140–180°F) or microwave.

AUSZOGENE

Ergibt ca. 12 Stück
Zubereitungszeit einschließlich Ruhezeit ca. 2,5 Stunden

Die Auszogene ist das klassische Schmalzgebäck Bayerns schlechthin. Man munkelt sogar, dass sie es bereits bis über den Großen Teich geschafft hat, um auf diversen amerikanischen »Oktoberfesten« die Gelüste der Besucher nach einer original bayerischen Süßigkeit zu befriedigen.
Der Name »Auszogene« weist auf die Herstellungsweise hin: Der Teig wird im Rohzustand auseinandergezogen, sodass im Inneren eine Art dünne »Teigmembran« entsteht, die sich beim Ausbacken nach oben wölbt. Manche behaupten, dass sich in früheren Zeiten die Hausfrau den Teig übers nackte Knie gezogen hat, um die charakteristische Form einer Auszogenen zu erhalten. Doch das ist historisch leider nicht bewiesen und fällt vermutlich in die Kategorie der bayerischen Sagen und Märchen.

ZUTATEN

FÜR DEN VORTEIG

ca. 30 g frische Hefe
1 Prise Zucker
1 EL Mehl
ca. 4 EL lauwarme Milch

BAVARIAN DOUGHNUTS

(PULLED PASTRY)

Yields about 12 pieces
Preparation time including resting time approx. 2.5 hours

The "Auszogene" (pulled pastry) is a classic deep-fried delicacy in Bavaria. It seems that several Oktoberfest celebrations in the US have started to offer it to satisfy the visitors craving traditional Bavarian sweets.
The name "Auszogene" comes from its manner of preparation. The raw dough is pulled apart so that a kind of membrane appears in the middle. This membrane then rises in a concave fashion while frying. It is said that in the old days, housewives would use their bare knees to stretch the dough and give this pastry its characteristic shape. This, however, has not been historically documented and, therefore, probably falls into the category of Bavarian sagas and fairy tales.

INGREDIENTS

FOR THE YEAST STARTER

1 oz yeast
1 pinch sugar
1 Tb flour
approx. 4 Tb lukewarm milk

FÜR DEN TEIG

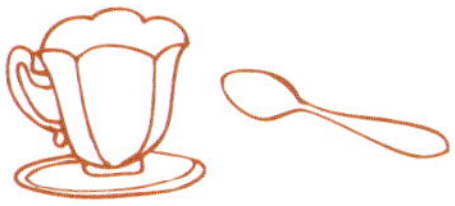

500 g Mehl
50 g Zucker
50 g zerlassene Butter
2 Eier
1 EL Obstler, z. B. Williamsbirne oder Kirschgeist
ca. 1/8 l lauwarme Milch
1 Prise Salz

AUSSERDEM heißes Fett zum Ausbacken, am besten ein Gemisch aus 500 g gehärtetem Pflanzenfett und 500 g Butterschmalz, Mehl zum Bestäuben der Arbeitsfläche, Küchentuch oder Küchenpapier zum Abtropfen

ZUBEREITUNG

Die Hefe zerbröckeln und in eine große Schüssel geben. Die restlichen Zutaten für den Vorteig zugeben und zu einer cremigen Masse verrühren. Dabei darauf achten, dass die Milch nicht zu heiß ist und dass Sie nicht zu viel Zucker beimengen – beides kann bewirken, dass der Teig nicht richtig aufgeht. Die Schüssel mit einem Küchentuch abdecken und ca. 15 Minuten lang an einem warmen, nicht zugigen Ort gehen lassen, bis dieses sogenannte »Dampferl« kleine Blasen geworfen hat.
Das Dampferl, sprich den Vorteig, nun zusammen mit Mehl, Zucker, Butter, Eiern und dem Obstler verrühren. Dann nach und nach die Milch zugeben und zu einem geschmeidigen Teig verkneten. Zum Schluss salzen und nochmals durchkneten. Zudecken und an einem warmen Ort 1 Stunde gehen lassen. Aufpassen, dass keine Zugluft an den Teig kommt.
Im Anschluss kleine Kugeln formen, etwa in der Größe von Golfbällen, auf die bemehlte Arbeitsfläche oder auf ein bemehltes Brett legen und mit Frischhaltefolie – sie verhindert eine Krustenbildung auf den Teigbällchen – und einem Küchentuch abdecken. Weitere 30 Minuten gehen lassen.
Nun die einzelnen Kugeln flach drücken und mit eingefetteten Fingern vorsichtig auseinanderziehen, sodass in der Mitte ein dünnes Teigfenster entsteht. Die Auszogene sollte ungefähr handtellergroß sein.
Einzeln ins heiße Fett gleiten lassen und 1–2 Mal mit etwas heißem Fett übergießen, damit sich das Teigfenster nach oben hin aufwölbt und blass bleibt. Auf einer Seite goldbraun ausbacken, dann vorsichtig wenden. Auch die andere Seite goldbraun backen und die Auszogene aus dem Fett nehmen. Auf ein sauberes Küchentuch oder Küchenpapier legen.
Je nach Geschmack die noch lauwarmen Auszogenen mit Puderzucker bestäuben oder »nackt« servieren.

FOR THE DOUGH

4 cups flour
3 Tb sugar
3 Tb melted butter
2 eggs
1 Tb fruit schnapps, e.g. a pear or cherry brandy
approx. 1/2 cup lukewarm milk
1 pinch salt

IN ADDITION hot fat for deep-frying, preferably a combination of 2 cups hardened vegetable fat and 2 cups clarified butter, flour for dusting work surface, kitchen towel or paper towel for straining

METHOD

Crumble the yeast into a bowl; add the remaining ingredients for the yeast starter and mix into a creamy paste. Make sure the milk is not too hot and you do not add too much sugar, since this might result in the yeast starter not rising as it should. Cover the bowl with a kitchen towel and place in a warm place without a draft for about 15 minutes. It is done rising when this "Dampferl," as it is called, forms little bubbles.
Now add the flour, sugar, butter, eggs and fruit schnapps to the yeast starter and blend well. Gradually add the milk and knead until it is a smooth consistency. Add the salt and knead once more. Cover and let rest in a warm spot for one hour. Make sure there is no draft.
Tear out pieces of the dough, forming balls the size of golf balls. Place these on a floured work surface or cutting board and cover with clear plastic wrap and a kitchen towel. This prevents a crust from developing. Let rest another 30 minutes.
Now flatten the balls and using your greased fingers carefully pull apart the dough in the middle forming a kind of membrane. The membrane in the middle of the dough disc should be so thin that you can almost see through it. The pulled pastries should be roughly palm-sized.
Gently let them glide into the hot fat one by one. Then pour hot fat over each one, twice if necessary, making the membrane rise and arch while remaining a pale color. Let the bottom side fry until golden and then carefully turn over. Fry the other side until golden and remove from fat. Set onto a paper towel or clean kitchen towel to drain.
Either sprinkle with powdered sugar when lukewarm or serve them plain.

FRÄNKISCHE NONNENFÜRZLE

Ergibt ca. 25 Stück
Zubereitungszeit inkl. Abkühlen des Teigs
1 Stunde 15 Minuten

Die Bezeichnung »Nonnenfurz« ist keineswegs eine Anspielung auf Anrüchiges, obwohl es auf den ersten Blick natürlich zu vermuten ist. Das Wort ist einigen historischen Quellen nach dem Mittelniederdeutschen »Nunnekenfurt« entlehnt und mit »von den Nonnen am besten zubereitet« zu übersetzen. Der spätere Wortschöpfer der »Nonnenfürzle« muss sich wohl einen Faschingsscherz erlaubt haben, denn die Nonnenfürze sind besonders zur »Fränkischen Fastnacht« beliebt.

ZUTATEN

250 ml Milch
1 Prise Salz
1 EL Butter
1 EL Zucker
2 TL (1 Pck.) Vanillezucker
250 g Mehl
3 Eier

AUSSERDEM heißes Fett zum Frittieren: je 500 g gehärtetes Pflanzenfett und Butterschmalz, Küchenpapier zum Abtropfen, Puderzucker zum Bestäuben

ZUBEREITUNG

Milch, Salz, Butter, Zucker und Vanillezucker zusammen in einen Topf geben und zum Kochen bringen. Anschließend das ganze Mehl auf einmal zugeben und kräftig mit einem Holzkochlöffel rühren, sodass ein zäher Teigklumpen entsteht. Während des Rührens den Herd bereits ausschalten, den Topf aber noch auf der Platte lassen. Der Brandteig ist fertig, wenn sich am Topfboden eine weiße Schicht gebildet hat.
Nun den Topf vom Herd nehmen und 1 Ei in den noch heißen Teig rühren. Den Teig in eine Schüssel geben und komplett auskühlen lassen. Erst dann die restlichen beiden Eier nacheinander mit den Händen einkneten, sodass ein zäher, klebriger Teig entsteht. Keine Sorge, wenn der Teig Klümpchen bildet, sie verschwinden beim Backen.
Das Fett zum Ausbacken erhitzen. Es ist zum Frittieren bereit, wenn sich am Stiel eines Holzkochlöffels, der in das heiße Fett

FRANCONIAN PUFF PASTRY

Yields about 25 puffs
Preparation time including cooling time approx.
1 hour and 15 minutes

The term “Nonnenfurz” (literally: nun’s fart) is not an allusion to something indecent, even if it seems that way at first glance. According to historians, it originates from the Middle Low German “Nunnekenfurt,” which means “best prepared by nuns.” Whoever coined the term “Nonnenfürzle” must have been making a small Fasching’s joke (carnival in Germany), since this pastry is especially popular during the “Fränkische Fastnacht” (Franconian carnival).

INGREDIENTS

1 cup milk
1 pinch salt
2 Tb butter
1 Tb sugar
2 tsp (1 sachet) vanilla sugar
2 cups flour
3 eggs

IN ADDITION hot fat for deep-frying, a combination of 2 cups hardened vegetable fat and 2 cups clarified butter, paper towels for draining, powdered sugar for dusting

METHOD

Place the milk, salt, butter, sugar and vanilla sugar in a pot and bring to a boil. Turn off the heat but keep the pot on the stove. Add all the flour at once and stir with a wooden spoon so that a stiff, heavy ball of dough results. The choux pastry is done as soon as a white layer forms on the bottom.
Remove pot from stove and stir in 1 egg. Place the dough in a bowl and let it cool completely. Only then add the remaining 2 eggs and knead with your hands until tough and sticky. Don’t worry if clumps form, they will disperse while baking.
Melt the clarified butter and vegetable shortening in a pot. Hold the handle of a wooden spoon into the fat to check if it is ready. If small bubbles form around the handle rising vertically, it is hot enough. Continue this process with the remaining dough. If the fat starts to bubble, turn down the heat. Let the puffs drain and cool on paper towels. Dust with powdered sugar.

gehalten wird, kleine Bläschen bilden, die senkrecht nach oben streben.
Mithilfe eines Teelöffels kleine Nocken ausstechen und portionsweise in das heiße Fett geben. Ca. 5–10 Minuten auf beiden Seiten goldgelb backen. So verfahren, bis der Teig aufgebraucht ist. Gegebenenfalls die Hitze reduzieren, wenn das Fett zu sehr aufkocht.
Die Nonnenfürzle auf Küchenpapier abtropfen und abkühlen lassen. Zum Schluss mit Puderzucker bestäuben.

HASENÖHRL

Ergibt ca. 40–50 Stück, je nach Größe
Zubereitungszeit insgesamt ca. 1 Stunde

In früheren Zeiten wurde dieses leckere Schmalzgebäck, das durch seine Rautenform tatsächlich entfernt an Hasenohren erinnert, auf vielen Bauernhöfen fast ausschließlich zu deftigen Suppen als Brotersatz gegessen. Es wurden immer gleich größere Mengen an Hasenöhrl zubereitet, denn es saßen damals nicht nur die Familie, sondern auch alle Bediensteten des Hofes mit am Tisch. Das erklärt auch die Mengenangaben dieses Originalrezepts, das Sie natürlich auch halbieren können. Lediglich das Ei lassen Sie weiterhin in seiner Ganzheit bestehen.
Vom Mittagessen übrig gebliebene Hasenöhrl schmecken wunderbar, mit Apfelmus zum Tunken, zum Nachmittagskaffee.

ZUTATEN

500 g Mehl
1 Msp. Backpulver
2 EL zerlassene Butter
300 g Sauerrahm
1 Ei
abgeriebene Schale von 1 unbehandelten Zitrone
ca. 75 ml kaltes Wasser

AUSSERDEM Mehl zum Bestäuben der Arbeitsfläche, heißes Fett zum Frittieren: ein Gemisch aus je 500 g gehärtetem Pflanzenfett und Butterschmalz, Küchenpapier zum Abtropfen, Puderzucker zum Bestäuben

ZUBEREITUNG

Mehl und Backpulver mischen und in eine große Schüssel sieben. Mit der zerlassenen Butter übergießen, dann die restlichen Zutaten nach und nach zugeben und zu einem glatten Teig verarbeiten. Die Arbeitsfläche mit Mehl bestäuben und den Teig messerrückendick ausrollen, danach in längliche Rauten schneiden.
Das Fett in einem großen Topf erhitzen. Um zu prüfen, ob das Fett die richtige Temperatur hat, halten Sie den Stiel eines Holzkochlöffels hinein. Wenn sich entlang des Stiels feine Bläschen bilden, können Sie loslegen! Die Teigrauten portionsweise 1–2 Minuten auf beiden Seiten goldbraun frittieren.
Die fertigen Hasenöhrl mit einer Schaumkelle aus dem Fett nehmen und auf Küchenpapier abtropfen lassen. Einen Teil mit Puderzucker bestäuben und lauwarm servieren, den Rest einfrieren.

RABBIT'S EARS

Yields 40–50 ears, depending on their individual size
Preparation time approx. 1 hour

This pastry gets its name from its rhombus shape, reminiscent of rabbit ears.
Back then it was common on many farms for this delicious fried pastry to substitute bread as a side for hearty soups. Copious amounts were made because not only the family sat at the dining table but all the servants of the farmyard as well. That is why this original recipe yields so much; you can, of course, halve all the ingredients' amounts if that suits you better. Only the amount of eggs stays the same.
Left over rabbit's ears from lunch are wonderful dunked in apple sauce to go with afternoon coffee.

INGREDIENTS

4 cups flour
1 small pinch baking powder
2 Tb melted butter
1 1/2 cups sour cream
1 egg
grated rind of 1 lemon
approx. 1/3 cup cold water

IN ADDITION flour for dusting work surface, hot fat for deep-frying, a combination of 2 cups hardened vegetable fat and 2 cups clarified butter, paper towels for draining, powdered sugar for dusting

METHOD

Mix the flour and baking powder sifting them into a bowl. Add the melted butter and then gradually, one by one, add the remaining ingredients kneading the dough until smooth. Flour the work surface and roll out the dough until about 1/2-inch thick. Cut out elongated rhombuses.
Melt the clarified butter and vegetable shortening in a pot. Hold the handle of a wooden spoon into the fat to check if it is ready. If small bubbles form around the handle rising vertically, it is hot enough for you to start frying. Fry each rhombus individually on either side for about 1–2 minutes until golden.
Remove the rabbit's ears from the fat with a skimmer and let them drain on a paper towel. Dust several pieces with powdered sugar and serve while lukewarm. Freeze the rest for later.

QUARKBÄLLCHEN

Ergibt ca. 40 Stück
Zubereitungszeit insgesamt ca. 1,5 Stunden

ZUTATEN

2 Eier
100 g Zucker
250 g Magerquark, 20% Fett i.Tr.
20 ml Rum, entspricht einem »Stamperl«
250 g Mehl
2 TL Backpulver

AUSSERDEM 500 g Butterschmalz und 500 g gehärtetes Pflanzenfett zum Ausbacken, Küchenpapier zum Abtropfen, Puderzucker zum Bestäuben

ZUBEREITUNG

Eier und Zucker cremig schlagen. Quark und Rum unterrühren. Mehl durch ein Sieb geben und das Backpulver beimengen. Mit der Masse zu einem klebrigen Teig verrühren.
Das Fett zum Ausbacken in einem Topf erhitzen. Um zu prüfen, ob es die richtige Temperatur hat, ein Holzstäbchen oder den Stiel eines Holzkochlöffels hineinhalten. Steigen kleine Bläschen am Holz entlang nach oben, ist das Fett heiß genug zum Frittieren. Darauf achten, dass es nicht zu heiß wird, bei Bedarf die Hitze reduzieren.
Mit einem Teelöffel kleine Bällchen ausstechen – Achtung, die Quarkbällchen gehen während des Frittierens auf, also nicht zu viele auf einmal in den Topf geben! – und im heißen Fett ca. 8–10 Minuten goldgelb backen. Auf einem Küchentuch abtropfen lassen. Portionsweise verfahren, bis der Teig aufgebraucht ist. Noch lauwarm mit Puderzucker bestäuben.

Tipp Frische, noch warme Quarkbällchen schmecken besonders gut mit Vanilleeis. Ausgekühlte oder aufgetaute Quarkbällchen – bei Niedrigtemperatur im Backofen erwärmt – lassen sich wunderbar in frisch aufgebrühten Kaffee tunken.

CURD CHEESE BALLS

Yields approx. 40 pieces
Preparation time approx. 1.5 hours

INGREDIENTS

2 eggs
1/2 cup sugar
1 cup low-fat curd cheese
4 tsp rum, is equivalent to a "schnapps"
2 cups flour
2 tsp baking powder

IN ADDITION 2 cups clarified butter and 2 cups of hardened vegetable fat for frying, kitchen paper to drain off, powdered sugar for dusting

METHOD

Beat the eggs and sugar together until creamy. Stir in curd cheese and rum. Sift flour through a sieve and add the baking soda. Mix with the mixture to make a sticky dough.
Heat the fat for frying in a pan. To check whether it has the correct temperature, dip a wooden chopstick or the handle of a wooden spoon in and if small blisters rise to the top of the wood, the fat is hot enough for frying. Make sure that it is not too hot, reduce the heat if necessary.
Cut out small balls with one teaspoon – warning, the curd cheese balls bloat during frying, do not place too many into the pot at once. Bake in the hot fat until golden yellow for about 8–10 minutes. Drain on a tea towel. Batches procedure, until the dough is used up. While still lukewarm dust with powdered sugar.

Tips & Hints Fresh, still warm curd cheese balls taste especially good with vanilla ice cream. Thawed or cooled off curd cheese balls – warmed in the oven at a low temperature – can be wonderful to dunk in freshly brewed coffee.

KIRCHWEIHNUDELN

Ergibt ca. 16 Stück
Zubereitungszeit inkl. Backzeit 35 Minuten +
1,5 Stunden Gehzeit

Kirchweih ist in Bayern ein hohes katholisches Kirchenfest, das traditionell am dritten Sonntag im Oktober gefeiert wird. Früher feierte jede Gemeinde ihre eigene Kirchweih, und zwar immer am Jahrestag des jeweiligen Kirchenpatrons. Im Jahr 1866 wurde aber die sogenannte »Allerweltskirchweih« eingeführt, der sich bis heute nur die Franken und die Oberpfälzer entziehen: Sie feiern immer noch mit Pomp und Gloria ihre Patrone zur gegebenen Zeit.
Die Kirchweihnudel hat an »Kirta«, wie das Fest umgangssprachlich genannt wird, einen festen Ehrenplatz auf den sich biegenden Festtafeln. Ebenso wie der Gänsebraten, das »Kirchweih-Ganserl«. Wegen ihres Aussehens, das im Idealfall einer Krone mit fünf »Zipfeln« gleicht, nennt man die Kirchweihnudel in manchen Gegenden auch »Zipfelnudel«.

ZUTATEN

FÜR DEN VORTEIG

30 g frische Hefe
ca. 4 EL lauwarmes Wasser
1 EL Mehl
1 Prise Zucker

FÜR DEN TEIG

500 g Mehl
60 g Butter, zimmerwarm
1/4 l Milch, zimmerwarm
125 g Sauerrahm, zimmerwarm
60 g Zucker
100 g Rosinen oder Sultaninen, mit etwas Mehl bestäubt
1 Prise Salz

AUSSERDEM 500 g gehärtetes Pflanzenfett und 500 g Butterschmalz zum Ausbacken, Küchenpapier oder Küchentuch zum Abtropfen, Puderzucker zum Bestäuben

ZUBEREITUNG

Alle Zutaten für den Vorteig in einer kleinen Schüssel miteinander vermengen und zugedeckt an einem warmen, nicht zugigen Ort ca. 30 Minuten gehen lassen.

DEDICATION PASTRY

Yields about 16 pieces
Preparation time including baking time 35 minutes +
1.5 hours resting time

When churches were built and consecrated, they were dedicated to a patron saint. This event began an important annual ritual. Dedication is a high Catholic celebration, traditionally celebrated on the third Sunday in October in Bavaria. Previously, each community celebrated their own dedication and always on its patron's anniversary. In 1866 the so-called "whole world consecration" was introduced, but the Franconia and the Upper Palatinate Bavarians still prefer celebrating their own patron saints with pomp and glory at the appointed time.
The dedication pastry has a fixed place of honor at the festive banquets of the "Kirta," as the Festival is known colloquially. Like the roast goose, the "Festival Ganserl," this specialty, the dedication pastry, is, in some areas, sometimes referred to as "Tines pastry" due to its appearance. Ideally it resembles a crown with five "tines."

INGREDIENTS

FOR THE YEAST STARTER

1 oz fresh yeast
approx. 4 Tb lukewarm water
1 Tb flour
1 pinch sugar

FOR THE DOUGH

4 cups flour
4 Tb butter at room temperature
1 cup milk at room temperature
5/8 cup sour cream at room temperature
5 Tb sugar
3 1/2 oz raisins or sultanas, dusted with flour
1 pinch salt

IN ADDITION 2 cups of hardened vegetable fat and 2 cups clarified butter for frying, paper towel or cloth to drip off, powdered sugar for dusting

METHOD

Mix all the ingredients for the yeast starter in a small bowl together and leave covered in a warm, draft-free place for 30 minutes.

Mehl in eine große Schüssel sieben und in die Mitte eine Mulde drücken. Den Vorteig in die Mulde geben. Butter, Milch, Sauerrahm, Zucker und Rosinen oder Sultaninen zugeben und alles gut miteinander verkneten. Erst zum Schluss das Salz zugeben und noch mal gut durchkneten, bis ein geschmeidiger Teig entsteht. Erneut zudecken und für eine weitere Stunde am gleichen Ort gehen lassen.
Anschließend aus dem Teig gleich große Stücke abstechen und daraus kleine Bälle mit ca. 3–4 cm Durchmesser formen. Zugedeckt weitere 15 Minuten gehen lassen.
Das Fett zum Ausbacken in einen großen Topf geben und erhitzen. Es hat die richtige Temperatur, wenn sich an dem hölzernen Stiel eines Kochlöffels, der ins Fett gehalten wird, kleine Bläschen bilden, die am Stiel entlang nach oben steigen. Während des Backens evtl. Hitze reduzieren, damit das Fett nicht zu heiß wird.
Jede Teigkugel mit einer Schere fünf Mal einschneiden, damit sich beim Frittieren die charakteristischen »Zipfel« bilden.
Die Nudeln portionsweise erst auf der einen, dann auf der anderen Seite goldbraun backen (insgesamt ca. 10–15 Minuten). Achten Sie darauf, nicht zu viele Nudeln gleichzeitig in den Topf zu geben; sie gehen in heißem Fett noch mal auf.
Die fertig gebackenen Kirchweihnudeln auf Küchentüchern oder Küchenpapier abtropfen und abkühlen lassen. Zum Servieren mit Puderzucker bestäuben. Sie schmecken besonders gut, wenn man sie zum Nachmittagskaffee in den heißen Milchkaffee tunkt. Das ist zwar nicht die feine englische, bzw. bayerische, Art, aber es schmeckt einfach himmlisch.

Tipp *Geben Sie in den Teig noch zusätzlich den Abrieb von einer unbehandelten Zitrone, das macht die Nudeln frischer. Und natürlich geht das Ganze auch pur, ohne Rosinen!*

Sift flour into a large bowl and make a hollow in the middle. Mold the yeast starter. Knead the butter, milk, sour cream, sugar and raisins or sultanas together. Finally add the salt and knead it well until a smooth dough is created. Cover again and leave for another hour in the same place.
Then cut equal pieces of the dough and form small balls approximately 1 1/2 inches in diameter. Cover and leave for 15 more minutes.
Heat the fat in a large pot for frying. It has the correct temperature, if you stick a wooden spoon in the fat, and it forms small blisters rising along the stick upwards. During baking, reduce any heat, so that the fat is not too hot.
Cut each dough ball five times with a pair of scissors so that the characteristic "pointy tines" are formed during frying.
Bake in batches only on one side then on the other side until golden (approx. 10–15 minutes). Make sure to add as many in one pot as possible and repeat in hot fat until dough is used.
Drain the finished baked dedication pastry on kitchen towels or paper towels and allow to cool. Serve with powdered sugar on top. They taste especially good when dunked in hot coffee with milk. While this is not the fine English or Bavarian style, nevertheless, it tastes divine.

Tips & Hints *Add the grated rind of an untreated lemon into the batter also, which makes the pastry stay fresh. And, of course, the whole thing is also delicious without raisins.*

SCHNEEBALLEN

Ergibt ca. 15 Stück
Zubereitungszeit ca. 40 Minuten + ca. 2 Stunden Ruhezeit

Der »Schneeball« – ursprünglich eine mittelfränkische Spezialität – ist ein traditionelles Schmalzgebäck, das in einigen Gegenden Bayerns neben der Kirchweihnudel (s. S. 50) speziell zur Kirchweih, einem wichtigen bayerischen Festtag, zubereitet wird. Aber auch zu Hochzeiten erfreut sich der »Schneeball« großer Beliebtheit, dann wird er allerdings kurzerhand, als Symbol für reichen Kindersegen, in »Storchennest« umbenannt.

ZUTATEN

3 Eier
50 g Zucker
2 TL (1 Pck.) Vanillezucker
2 EL Sonnenblumenöl
2 EL Sahne
nach Belieben 2 EL Kirschwasser oder Williamsbirne zum Verfeinern des Teigs
350 g Mehl, gesiebt

AUSSERDEM Sonnenblumenöl zum Bestreichen des Teigs, zum Ausbacken: 500 g Butterschmalz und 500 g gehärtetes Pflanzenfett, Küchenpapier zum Abtropfen, Puderzucker zum Bestäuben

ZUBEREITUNG

Eier, Zucker, Vanillezucker, Sonnenblumenöl und Sahne in einer Schüssel miteinander verrühren. Falls gewünscht, Kirschwasser oder Williamsbirne unterrühren. Nach und nach Mehl zugeben und so lange kneten, bis ein fester Teig entsteht. Die Teigkugel mit Sonnenblumenöl bestreichen und zugedeckt ca. 2 Stunden ruhen lassen.
Zum Weiterverarbeiten werden walnussgroße Stücke aus dem Teig gerissen und mit dem Nudelholz zu hauchdünnen Teigstücken ausgerollt, etwa in der Größe eines Kuchentellers. Erst wenn man durch den Teig hindurch quasi die Zeitung lesen könnte – ähnlich wie beim Strudelteig –, ist er perfekt.
Nun jedes der »Teigblätter« in der Mitte parallel in 5–6 Steifen schneiden, wobei außen bzw. rundherum ein ca. 1 cm breiter Rand bleiben muss.
Nebenher Schmalz und Pflanzenfett in einen großen Topf geben und erhitzen. Ist das Fett heiß genug – an einem ins Fett

SNOWBALLS

Yields about 15 snowballs
Preparation time approx. 40 minutes + approx. 2 hours resting time

The snowball was originally a Middle Franconian specialty, a traditional deep-fried pastry. In some parts of Bavaria, it shares the honors with the "Kirchweihnudel" (see pg. 50) at the "Kirchweih" (a parish fair or church-consecration celebration), which is a major religious holiday in Bavaria. The snowball also enjoys immense/great popularity at weddings. However, as a symbol of fertility it is served at weddings as the "Storchennest" (literally: stork's nest).

INGREDIENTS

3 eggs
scant 1/4 cup sugar
2 tsp (1 sachet) vanilla sugar
2 Tb sunflower oil
2 Tb cream
to taste: 2 Tb cherry or williams pear brandy to enhance flavor
approx. 2 4/5 cups sifted flour

IN ADDITION sunflower oil for brushing the dough, 2 cups clarified butter and 2 cups hardened vegetable fat for deep frying, paper towels for draining, powdered sugar for dusting

METHOD

Mix the eggs, sugar, vanilla sugar, sunflower oil and cream together in a bowl. Add cherry or pear brandy to taste if desired. Gradually knead in the flour until the dough is firm and supple. Form a ball of dough; brush with sunflower oil, cover and let rest for about 2 hours.
Now tear off walnut-sized pieces of dough and roll them out paper-thin with a rolling pin to create a disk approximately the size of a dessert plate. As with strudel, the dough should be so thin that you can almost read a newspaper through it; only then is the snowball really ready for frying. Take care to leave about a 1/2-inch edge and cut 5–6 parallel slits in the center of the disk of dough with a pastry cutter.
Melt the clarified butter and vegetable shortening in a pot. Hold the handle of a wooden spoon into the fat. If small bubbles form around the handle, it is hot enough and the disks can be

gehaltenen Holzkochlöffelstiel steigen Bläschen auf –, die Teigstreifen eines der Teigstücke einzeln mit dem Stiel eines Kochlöffels aufnehmen und das ganze Gebilde vorsichtig in den Topf geben. Erst im heißen Fett zieht sich der Teig zu einem Ball zusammen. Portionsweise so verfahren und einen Schneeball nach dem anderen einzeln ausbacken. Schneeballen werden nur sehr kurz gebacken, denn sie sollen lediglich eine leicht goldene Färbung annehmen. Mit einer Schaumkelle aus dem Topf nehmen und auf einem Küchentuch abtropfen lassen. Noch warm mit Puderzucker bestäuben.

added one by one. Insert the spoon's handle in the slits made earlier, carefully lifting the snowball and placing it in the fat. The disks contract into a ball all by themselves as soon as they come into contact with the hot fat. Repeat this process with the rest of the dough. Make sure you fry each snowball separately. Fry the snowballs only until they have turned a light golden color and then using a skimmer transfer them to a paper towel to drain. Sprinkle with powdered sugar while still warm.

SCHUX'N

Ergibt ca. 30 Stück
Zubereitungszeit inkl. Backzeit 45 Minuten + insgesamt 4 Stunden Ruhezeit für den Teig

Streng genommen heißt dieses Schmalzgebäck »Schuchse«, aber umgangssprachlich findet man in Bayern oft das gesprochene »x« statt dem »ch«. Die korrekt geschriebene »Schuchse« leitet sich einer Überlieferung nach von dem Wort »Schuhsohle« ab. Demnach ist das im Fett ausgebackene Gebäck im Idealfall exakt so lang wie die Schuhsohle eines ausgewachsenen Mannes.
Manche mögen sich fragen, warum so ein simples Schmalzgebäck Einzug in dieses Buch gefunden hat. Nun, viele alte, überlieferte Rezepte fallen sonst dem Vergessen anheim, und die Schux'n ist so ein Kandidat dafür – kommt sie von den Zutaten doch recht ärmlich daher. In früheren Zeiten aß man sie eher zu deftigen Gerichten als Brotersatz, und war mal etwas Zucker, der bei armen Bauern als kostbar galt, im Haus, dann streute man diesen reichlich darüber und genoss seine Schux'n zur nachmittäglichen Kaffeepause. Trotzdem waren die Schux'n kein alltägliches Gericht; in manchen Gegenden Bayerns waren sie ausschließlich hohen kirchlichen Feiertagen vorbehalten. So aß man sie zum Beispiel entlang der Alpen nur am 6. Januar, dem Dreikönigstag.

ZUTATEN

300 g Roggenmehl, Type 1150
1/8 l Milch
250 g Magerquark, 20% Fett i. Tr.
1 Prise Salz

AUSSERDEM etwas Roggenmehl für die Arbeitsfläche, Nudelholz, zum Ausbacken: 250 g Butterschmalz und 250 g gehärtetes Pflanzenfett, Küchenpapier zum Abtropfen, Puderzucker zum Bestreuen

ZUBEREITUNG

Die Hälfte des Mehls in eine Schüssel geben und mit der Milch zu einem festen Teig kneten. Die Schüssel mit einem Tuch abdecken und den Teig 3 Stunden ruhen lassen.
Dann den Rest des Mehls, Quark und Salz zugeben und das Ganze wieder zu einem glatten, geschmeidigen Teig kneten. Da das Roggenmehl sehr klebt, ist es ratsam, die Hände immer wieder mit kaltem Wasser zu benetzen. Den Teig erneut abdecken und 1 weitere Stunde ruhen lassen.

FRIED DOUGH BREAD

("SCHUX'N")

Yields about 30 pieces
Preparation time including baking time 45 minutes + 4 hours resting time for the dough

This cake is strictly speaking spelled "Schuchse," but colloquially it is often pronounced with an "x" instead of the "ch" sound in Bavaria. According to tradition, the correctly written "Schuchse" is derived from the word "Shoe sole." Therefore, ideally, these pastries baked in fat were as long as the sole of a full-grown man.
Some may wonder how such a simple cake has found its way into this book; many much older, more traditional recipes are otherwise forgotten, especially when the ingredients are pretty simple and cheap – which makes the "Schux'n" a perfect candidate. In the past, it was a rather hearty dish used as a bread substitute, and sometimes, when poor farmers had some sugar in the house, something considered precious, they sprinkled it over their "Schux'n" and enjoyed them during the afternoon coffee break. Yet the "Schux'n" were no ordinary meal; in some areas of Bavaria, they were reserved exclusively for High Church holidays. So you ate them, for example, in the region flanking the Alps only on January 6, the Epiphany.

INGREDIENTS

3 1/3 cups rye flour type 1150
1/2 cup milk
1 cup low-fat curd cheese
1 pinch salt

IN ADDITION some rye flour for the work surface, rolling pin, for frying: 1 cup clarified butter and 1 cup hardened vegetable fat, kitchen paper to drain off, powdered sugar for sprinkling

METHOD

Sift half of the flour in a bowl and knead with the milk to make a firm dough. Cover the bowl with a cloth and let the dough rest for 3 hours.
Then add the rest of the flour, curd cheese and salt and knead the whole thing again until a smooth, supple dough. As rye flour is very sticky, it is advisable to wet your hands with cold water repeatedly. Cover the dough again and let it rest for 1 more hour.

Das Fett in einen Topf geben und erhitzen. Es ist bereit zum Ausbacken, wenn am Stiel eines hölzernen Kochlöffels, den Sie ins heiße Fett tauchen, kleine Bläschen senkrecht nach oben steigen.
Den Teig aus der Schüssel nehmen und zu einem dicken, länglichen Strang rollen. In ca. 3 mm dicke Scheiben portionieren.
Arbeitsfläche mit Mehl bestäuben und die Teigscheiben mit dem Nudelholz messerrückendick ausrollen. Portionsweise von beiden Seiten im heißen Fett ausbacken, bis sie goldbraun sind. Sie blähen sich beim Frittieren auf und bilden einen Hohlraum. Die »Außenhaut« ist sehr zart.
Auf Küchenpapier abtropfen lassen und noch lauwarm mit reichlich Puderzucker bestäuben. Pur genossen, haben die Schux'n einen leicht herben Geschmack, der für unsere modernen Geschmacksknospen vielleicht etwas gewöhnungsbedürftig ist.

Melt the fat in a pan. It is ready for frying when you dip the handle of a wooden spoon into the hot fat and small bubbles rise vertically upwards.
Take the dough out of the bowl and roll to a thick, elongated strand. Portion in approximately 1/10 inches thick slices.
Dust work surface with flour and roll out the dough disks with the rolling pin about as thick as the back of the knife. Fry in batches on both sides in the hot oil until they are golden brown. They bloat when frying and form a cavity. The "outer" skin is very tender.
Drain on paper towels and dust with plenty of powdered sugar while still lukewarm. Properly enjoyed the "Schux'n" have a slightly tart flavor that perhaps takes a little getting used to for our modern taste buds.

Kuchen & Torten

Cakes & Pies

ALM-KÄSEKUCHEN

Zubereitungszeit ca. 40 Minuten + mindestens 2 Stunden Kühlzeit für den Teig + ca. 75 Minuten Backzeit

Dieses Rezept ist eigentlich streng geheim. Ich habe es mir trotzdem über ein paar Ecken besorgen können und gnade mir Gott, wenn dies jemals der Erfinder des Käsekuchens – und gleichzeitig der Betreiber jener Alm, auf der er fast täglich serviert wird – herausbekommt. Ich habe schon so manchen Gast in seiner Küche betteln sehen, aber der Wirt ist immer standhaft geblieben. Aus diesem Grund nenne ich auch nicht den Namen der Alm, auch wenn sie ein wirklich schönes Ausflugsziel in den bayerischen Bergen ist und der Kuchen sogar nach ihr benannt wurde. Belassen wir es also bei der schnöden Bezeichnung Alm-Käsekuchen, hinter der sich ein wahrhaft köstliches Meisterwerk verbirgt.

ZUTATEN

FÜR DEN TEIG

250 g Mehl
75 g Puderzucker
125 g kalte Butter
1 großes Ei, kalt aus dem Kühlschrank
1 EL Rum
1 Prise Salz

FÜR DIE FÜLLUNG

125 g Butter
200 g Zucker
2 TL (1 Pck.) Vanillezucker
5 Eigelb
1 EL Grieß
250 g Quark, 40% Fett i. Tr.
1 EL Sahne
500 g Magerquark, 20% Fett i. Tr.
Saft von 1 Zitrone
6 Eiweiß, mit 1 Prise Salz steif geschlagen

AUSSERDEM Frischhaltefolie, Springform, 26 cm Durchmesser, etwas Butter und Mehl zum Einfetten und Ausmehlen der Form

ZUBEREITUNG

Mehl und Puderzucker in eine Schüssel geben. Butter in kleine Flöckchen schneiden. Alle Zutaten für den Teig zu einem glatten Mürbeteigball verkneten. Darauf achten, dass Sie den

ALM-CHEESECAKE

Preparation time approx. 40 minutes + minimum 2 hours cooling time for the dough + approx.75 minutes baking time

This recipe is actually top secret. I was nevertheless able to enjoin its inventor to reveal the makings of this famous cheesecake – and God help me if he finds out that I've passed it on. He operates a small Alpine restaurant, and it is served there almost daily. I've seen many guests begging him for the recipe in his kitchen, but he has remained steadfast and tight-lipped and that is why business too has remained steadfast. For this reason, I will not mention the mountain where the restaurant is located, even if it is a really beautiful destination in the Bavarian mountains – because the cake named after it. Let's just restrict ourselves to the traditional and original name "Alm-Cheesecake," a truly delicious masterpiece.

INGREDIENTS

FOR THE DOUGH

2 cups flour
1/3 cup powdered sugar
8 Tb cold butter
1 large egg, cold from the fridge
1 Tb rum
1 pinch salt

FOR THE FILLING

8 Tb butter
1 cup sugar
2 tsp (1 sachet) vanilla sugar
5 egg yolks
1 Tb semolina
1 cup curd cheese
1 Tb cream
2 cups low-fat curd cheese
juice of 1 lemon
6 stiffly beaten egg whites with a pinch of salt

IN ADDITION clear plastic wrap, spring form pan, 10 inches in diameter, some butter and flour for greasing

METHOD

Mix the flour and powdered sugar in a bowl. Cut butter into small cubes. Knead all the ingredients for the dough into a smooth ball of pastry. Make sure that you do not knead the

Teig nicht zu lange kneten und dass sowohl die Butter als auch das Ei wirklich kalt, also frisch aus dem Kühlschrank sind. In Frischhaltefolie einpacken und mindestens 2 Stunden – am besten jedoch über Nacht – im Kühlschrank ruhen lassen.
Für die Füllung Butter, Zucker, Vanillezucker und Eigelbe cremig schlagen. Grieß unterrühren. Den Quark (40% Fett i. Tr.) mit Sahne verrühren und zur Masse geben. Dann nacheinander die restlichen Zutaten unterrühren. Zum Schluss das steif geschlagene Eiweiß vorsichtig unterheben.
Backofen auf 180 Grad vorheizen.
Den Teig aus dem Kühlschrank nehmen und dünn ausrollen. Das geht besonders gut zwischen zwei Lagen Frischhaltefolie, aber es klappt auch ohne!
Die Springform gut mit Butter einfetten und anschließend mit Mehl rundum bestäuben. Den Mürbeteig einlegen, dabei die Ränder bis ganz nach oben ziehen.
Die Käsekuchenmasse einfüllen und den Kuchen ca. 75 Minuten backen. Der Käsekuchen ist fertig, wenn seine Oberfläche »aufreißt« und insgesamt goldbraun und am Rand etwas dunkler geworden ist. Manchmal bildet sich in der Mitte auch eine Art Kuhle – für unseren oben genannten Wirt ein untrügliches Zeichen dafür, dass der Käsekuchen aus dem Ofen muss.

Tipp *Die Masse wird erst beim Abkühlen wirklich fest; beim Herausnehmen des Kuchens aus dem Backrohr »wackelt« das Ganze noch recht bedrohlich. Lassen Sie sich davon nicht einschüchtern, das muss so sein. Grundsätzlich gilt beim Käsekuchen: Lieber etwas zu weich aus dem Ofen nehmen, als zu lange backen!*

dough too long and that both the butter and the egg are really cold, i.e. fresh from the refrigerator. Wrap in plastic wrap and let rest for at least 2 hours – best however overnight – in the refrigerator.
For the filling, beat butter, sugar, vanilla sugar and egg yolks until creamy. Stir in flour. Mix the the curd cheese and add it to the mixture. Then stir in the remaining ingredients. Carefully stir in the stiffly beaten egg whites at the end.
Preheat the oven to 350°F.
Take the dough out of the refrigerator and roll out thinly. That works particularly well between two layers of plastic wrap, but it also works well without.
Grease the spring form pan well with butter and then sprinkle with flour around. Insert the shortcrust pastry, pulling the edges all the way up.
Fill with the cheesecake mixture and bake the cake for about 75 minutes. The cheesecake is ready when its surface "crackles" and sort of "disintegrates" and turns golden brown all over and the edges of the cake begin to darken. Sometimes also a kind of sunken hollow forms in the middle – for our above unnamed mountain restaurateur an unmistakable sign that the cheesecake is done and should be taken out of the oven.

Tips & Hints *The consistency only becomes really solid after it has cooled; when removing the cake from the oven, it is still quite jiggly and sometimes feels almost a bit pudding-mushy. Don't worry; it is supposed to be like this. The basic baking rule for cheesecake reads: better a bit too soft upon removal from the oven than in there too long.*

ALTBAYERISCHER APFEL-SCHOKO-KUCHEN

Zubereitungszeit ca. 25 Minuten + Backzeit ca. 50 Minuten

ZUTATEN

250 g Butter, zimmerwarm
200 g Zucker
2 TL (1 Pck.) Vanillezucker
4 Eigelb
200 g Mehl
2 TL Backpulver
100 g gemahlene Haselnüsse
2 EL Kakaopulver
1/2 TL Zimt
4 Eiweiß, mit 1 Prise Salz steif geschlagen
500 g säuerliche Äpfel, geschält, vom Kerngehäuse befreit, geviertelt und in Scheiben geschnitten

AUSSERDEM 1 Springform, 26 cm Durchmesser, etwas Butter und Mehl zum Einfetten und Ausstäuben der Form

ZUBEREITUNG

Butter, Zucker, Vanillezucker und Eigelbe in eine Schüssel geben und gut miteinander verrühren. Dann nach und nach Mehl, Backpulver, Haselnüsse, Kakaopulver und Zimt zugeben und gut miteinander zu einem eher festen, zähen Rührteig verarbeiten. Zum Schluss den Eischnee kräftig unterrühren, sodass die Teigmasse eine lockere Konsistenz annimmt.
Backofen auf 170 Grad vorheizen.
Den Teig in die eingefettete und mit etwas Mehl ausgestäubte Springform füllen und glatt streichen. Äpfel gleichmäßig darauf verteilen und den Kuchen ca. 50 Minuten backen. Stäbchenprobe machen!

Tipps

* *Variieren Sie mit dem Obst: Sie können statt der Äpfel z. B. auch die gleiche Menge Sauerkirschen oder Aprikosen nehmen.*
* *2–3 EL Marmelade, z. B. Aprikosen- oder Erdbeermarmelade, im Rührteig machen den Kuchen noch saftiger.*
* *Ohne das Kakaopulver im Teig wird der Altbayerische Apfel-Schoko-Kuchen zu einem schlichten hellen Apfelkuchen, der auch sehr lecker schmeckt.*

OLD BAVARIAN APPLE CHOCOLATE CAKE

Preparation time approx. 25 minutes + baking time approx. 50 minutes

INGREDIENTS

1/2 lb butter at room temperature
1 cup sugar
2 tsp (1 sachet) vanilla sugar
4 egg yolks
1 3/5 cups flour
2 tsp baking powder
1 cup ground hazelnuts
2 Tb cocoa powder
1/2 tsp cinnamon
4 stiffly beaten egg whites with a pinch of salt
3 cups tart apples, peeled, freed from the core, quartered and sliced

IN ADDITION 1 spring form pan, 10 inches in diameter, some butter and flour to grease and dust

METHOD

Mix butter, sugar, vanilla sugar and egg yolks in a bowl and stir well. Then gradually add flour, baking powder, hazelnuts, cocoa powder and cinnamon, till worked into a thick, tough sponge dough. Finally stir in the egg whites vigorously, so that the dough develops a loose, light consistency.
Preheat the oven to 350°F.
Fill the dough into the greased and floured spring form pan. Spread apples evenly over the dough and bake the cake for approximately 50 minutes. Skewer test.

Tips & Hints

* *Vary with the fruit: Instead of apples you can also use the same amount of sour cherries or apricots.*
* *2–3 Tb jam, such as apricot or strawberry jam, in the batter can make the cake juicier.*
* *The Bavarian apple cake can also be made without the cocoa powder in the dough to form a simple bright apple pie, which is also very tasty.*

APFELKUCHEN

Zubereitungszeit inkl. Backzeit ca. 1 Stunde

ZUTATEN

125 g Butter, zimmerwarm
100 g Zucker
2 TL (1 Pck.) Vanillezucker
1 Prise Salz
Abrieb von 1 unbehandelten Zitrone
3 Eier
200 g Mehl
2 TL Backpulver
2 EL Aprikosenkonfitüre
1 EL Milch
750 g säuerliche Äpfel, geschält, vom Kerngehäuse befreit, geviertelt und auf den Oberflächen der Länge nach mehrfach eingeritzt

AUSSERDEM 1 Springform, 26 cm Durchmesser, etwas Butter und Semmelbrösel (oder Mehl) zum Einfetten und Ausstäuben der Form, 100 g Aprikosenkonfitüre und Saft von 1/2 Zitrone zum Glasieren des fertigen Kuchens

ZUBEREITUNG

Backofen auf 180 Grad vorheizen.
Alle Zutaten bis auf die Äpfel für den Teig nacheinander in einer Schüssel zu einem zähen Rührteig verarbeiten. Den Teig gleichmäßig in der eingefetteten und ausgestäubten Springform verteilen. Äpfel sternförmig auf dem Teig verteilen. Den Kuchen in ca. 45 Minuten goldbraun backen – Stäbchenprobe machen!
Auskühlen lassen.
Aprikosenkonfitüre zusammen mit dem Zitronensaft erhitzen, bis die Konfitüre flüssig ist. Mit einem Pinsel die Oberfläche des Kuchens gleichmäßig damit bestreichen.

Tipp Das Bestreichen des Kuchens mit Aprikosenmarmelade bewirkt, dass er schön saftig bleibt. Sie können Ihren Apfelkuchen aber nach dem Erkalten auch mit Puderzucker bestäuben.

APPLE PIE

Preparation time including baking time approx. 1 hour

INGREDIENTS

8 Tb butter at room temperature
1/2 cup sugar
2 tsp (1 sachet) vanilla sugar
1 pinch salt
grated rind of 1 untreated lemon
3 eggs
1 3/5 cups flour
2 tsp baking powder
2 Tb apricot jam
1 Tb milk
4 cups tart apples, peeled, freed from the core, quartered and repeatedly carved on the surface lengthwise

IN ADDITION 1 spring form pan, 10 inches in diameter, some butter and breadcrumbs (or flour) to grease and dust the pan, 100 g apricot jam and juice of 1/2 a lemon to glaze the finished cake

METHOD

Preheat the oven to 350°F.
Mix all the ingredients for the dough – except for the apples – in a bowl to form a tough sponge dough. Distribute the dough into the greased and dusted springform. Spread star-shaped apples over the dough. Bake the cake for about 45 minutes until golden brown – use skewer to test.
Allow to cool off.
Together with the lemon juice, heat apricot jam, until the jam is liquid. Using a brush, evenly coat the surface of the cake.

Tips & Hints The coating with apricot jam on the cake allows it to stay juicy. You can sprinkle your apple pie with powdered sugar when it has cooled.

GUGLHUPF

Zubereitungszeit ca. 15 Minuten + Ruhezeit insgesamt 1 Stunde + Backzeit ca. 45 Minuten

Die Wiege des Guglhupf steht eigentlich in Österreich. Er ist ein Klassiker unter den österreichischen Mehlspeisen und tatsächlich ist nachstehendes Rezept auch unter dem Namen »Wiener Guglhupf« bekannt; es besticht durch seine Einfachheit und kommt mit sehr wenigen, aber feinen Zutaten aus.

ZUTATEN

FÜR DEN VORTEIG

30 g Hefe
1–2 EL Mehl
ca. 6 EL lauwarmes Wasser
1 Prise Zucker

FÜR DEN TEIG

250 g Butter, zimmerwarm
5 Eier, zimmerwarm
6 EL Zucker
2 TL (1 Pck.) Vanillezucker
ca. 500 g Mehl, gesiebt
200 g Sultaninen, ungeschwefelt
1 Prise Salz

AUSSERDEM 1 Guglhupfform, Butter oder Margarine zum Einfetten der Form, Puderzucker zum Bestäuben des Kuchens

ZUBEREITUNG

Die Zutaten für den Vorteig in eine kleine Schüssel geben und zu einer cremigen Masse verrühren. Mit einem Küchentuch bedecken und ca. 15 Minuten lang an einem warmen, nicht zugigen Ort gehen lassen.
Anschließend Butter, Eier, Zucker und Vanillezucker in einer separaten Schüssel schaumig rühren. Das Mehl zugeben und unterrühren. Dann den Vorteig und die Sultaninen zufügen und untermischen. Eine Prise Salz dazugeben und den Teig gut durchkneten.
Die Guglhupfform einfetten und den Teig einfüllen. Das Ganze erneut mit einem Küchentuch bedecken und an einem warmen, nicht zugigen Ort gehen lassen. Der Teig sollte dabei sein Volumen verdoppeln, das dauert ca. 30–40 Minuten.

BUNDT CAKE

Preparation time approx. 15 minutes + total resting time approx. 1 hour + baking time approx. 45 minutes

The "Guglhupf" actually originated in Austria where it has become a classic. As a matter of fact, the recipe that follow is also known as "Wiener Guglhupf" (literally: "Viennese bundt cake"). The beauty of this cake lies in its simplicity; just a few select ingredients are all that is needed to turn out a masterpiece.

INGREDIENTS

FOR THE YEAST STARTER

1 oz yeast
1–2 Tb flour
approx. 6 Tb lukewarm water
1 pinch sugar

FOR THE DOUGH

1/2 lb butter at room temperature
5 eggs at room temperature
6 Tb sugar
2 tsp (1 sachet) vanilla sugar
approx. 4 cups flour, sifted
1 cup sultanas, unsulfured
1 pinch salt

IN ADDITION 1 bundt cake pan, butter or margarine for greasing the pan, powdered sugar for dusting

METHOD

Put the ingredients for the yeast starter in a bowl and beat into a creamy paste. Cover with a kitchen towel and let rest in a warm spot without a draft for 15 minutes.
Beat the butter, eggs, sugar and vanilla sugar in a separate bowl until foamy. Add the sifted flour to the egg mixture. Add the yeast starter and raisins and combine. Add a pinch of salt and knead the dough thoroughly.
Grease the bundt pan and pour in the dough. Cover with a kitchen towel and place in a warm spot – without a draft – to rise. Wait until the volume has doubled, this takes approximately 30–40 minutes.
Preheat oven to 400°F.
Bake the "Guglhupf" for approximately 45 minutes. Test with a skewer. After the bundt cake has finished baking, let it cool down and then dust with powdered sugar.

Den Backofen auf 200 Grad vorheizen. Den Guglhupf ca. 45 Minuten im Rohr backen. Stäbchenprobe machen! Nach dem Backen und Auskühlen mit Puderzucker bestäuben.

Tipps

- *Machen Sie es wie die Engländer mit ihren frischen Scones zur »Tea-Time«: Geben Sie auf eine frische, noch warme Scheibe Guglhupf einen Klacks Sahne (besser und stilvoller ist allerdings noch die traditionelle Clotted Cream) und etwas Erdbeerkonfitüre – ein Genuss!*
- *Sehr lecker schmeckt ofenwarmer Guglhupf auch mit frischer Butter bestrichen.*

Tips & Hints

- *Try doing it as the English do with their fresh scones at teatime. Serve a slice of "Guglhupf" warm from the oven with a dollop of whipped cream (the traditional clotted cream, however, tastes better and has more style) and some strawberry jam – a delight.*
- *This cake is also delicious when served warm and spread with butter.*

BIERKUCHEN

Zubereitungszeit ca. 10 Minuten + Backzeit ca. 60–90 Minuten + 2 Wochen Ruhezeit vor dem Verzehr

Dieser Kuchen braucht viel Geduld, allerdings in Sachen Warten und nicht beim Zubereiten. Er muss nämlich so richtig schön durchziehen – je länger, desto besser!

ZUTATEN

100 g Butter, zimmerwarm
250 g Zucker
2 Eier
300 g Mehl, gesiebt
1 TL Natron
100 g Zitronat
50 g Orangeat
200 g Sultaninen
1 TL Zimtpulver
1 EL Kakaopulver
250 ml dunkles Bier

AUSSERDEM 200 g dunkle Kuvertüre für die Glasur, 1 große Kastenform, Butter zum Einfetten der Form, Alufolie

ZUBEREITUNG

Den Backofen auf 200 Grad vorheizen.
Butter mit Zucker in einer großen Schüssel schaumig schlagen, anschließend alle weiteren Zutaten für den Teig nach und nach zugeben und gut miteinander verrühren.
Die Kastenform mit reichlich Butter einfetten, dann den Rührteig gleichmäßig einfüllen. Ca. 60–90 Minuten backen. Stäbchenprobe machen!
Bevor Sie den Kuchen stürzen, lassen Sie ihn ein paar Minuten in der Form abkühlen.
Während dieser Zeit Wasser in einem kleinen Topf erhitzen, Kuvertüre in Stücke brechen und in einer Schüssel über dem Wasserdampf schmelzen. Dabei darauf achten, dass der Boden der Schüssel nicht mit dem Topfboden in Berührung kommt.
Mit der noch heißen Kuvertüre den Bierkuchen glasieren. Ist die Glasur trocken, wird der Kuchen mit einem Küchentuch bedeckt, damit er über Nacht komplett auskühlen kann. Dann fest in Alufolie einwickeln und zwei Wochen an einem kühlen und trockenen Ort ruhen lassen.

BEER CAKE

Preparation time approx. 10 minutes + baking time approx. 60–90 minutes + 2 weeks rest period before consumption

This cake requires quite a bit of patience, but only in terms of waiting, not making. Namely, it needs to set in order to become richly aromatic, fully absorb all the flavors, the longer, the better.

INGREDIENTS

7 Tb butter at room temperature
1 cup sugar
2 eggs
2 2/5 cups flour, sifted
1 tsp baking soda
3 1/2 oz candied lemon peel
2 oz candied orange peel
1 cup sultanas
1 tsp cinnamon powder
1 Tb cocoa powder
1 cup dark beer

IN ADDITION 7 oz dark chocolate for the icing, 1 large loaf form, butter for greasing the form, aluminum foil

METHOD

Preheat the oven to 400°F.
Stir butter with sugar in a large bowl until foamy, then gradually add all the other ingredients for the dough and mix well.
Grease loaf form with plenty of butter, then fill the batter evenly into the form. Bake for approximately 60–90 minutes. Insert toothpick to test firmness.
Before removing the cake, let it cool a few minutes in the form.
In the meantime, heat water in a small saucepan, break chocolate into pieces and melt in a bowl over the water vapor. Make sure that the bottom of the bowl does not touch the water in the bottom of the pot.
Glaze the beer cake with the hot chocolate. Once the glaze is dry, cover the cake with a kitchen towel and let it cool completely overnight. Then wrap firmly in aluminum foil and let it rest for two weeks in a cool, dry place.

DONAUWELLEN

Zubereitungszeit inkl. Backzeit ca. 1 Stunde

Ob die süße Donauwelle tatsächlich eine rein bayerische Erfindung ist, wage ich zu bezweifeln, aber da sich dieser majestätische Fluss auch durch einen großen Teil des Freistaats schlängelt, muss das Rezept dieses leckeren Kuchens unbedingt auf diesen Seiten seinen Einzug finden.
Woher die Welle ihren Namen hat, ist nicht bekannt. Mit viel Fantasie erinnern jedenfalls die beiden übereinanderliegenden Teigböden – der eine hell, der andere dunkel – an ein fließendes Gewässer in seinem sandigen Bett, mitsamt den Kirschen als Flusskiesel.
In manchen Gebieten Deutschlands wird die Donauwelle auch »Schneewittchenkuchen« genannt, eben weil sie »weiß wie Schnee, rot wie Blut und schwarz wie Ebenholz« ist.

ZUTATEN

FÜR DEN TEIG

250 g Butter, zimmerwarm
180 g Zucker
6 Eier
1 Prise Salz
400 g Mehl
2 TL Backpulver
3 EL Milch
3 EL Kakaopulver
700 g Schattenmorellen aus dem Glas, abgetropft

FÜR DIE CREME

1 Pck. Vanillepuddingpulver
1/2 l Milch
80 g Puderzucker
250 g Butter, zimmerwarm

AUSSERDEM 1 kleines, tiefes Backblech, Butter zum Einfetten des Blechs, 300 g Zartbitterkuvertüre

ZUBEREITUNG

Backofen auf 200 Grad vorheizen.
Butter mit Zucker in einer Schüssel schaumig schlagen. Eier nach und nach unterrühren. Dann Salz, Mehl und Backpulver zugeben und alles zu einem zähen Rührteig verarbeiten. Die Hälfte des Teigs auf das eingefettete Backblech geben und gleichmäßig verstreichen. Zum Rest des Teigs in der Schüssel

DANUBE RIVER WAVES

Preparation time including baking time approx. 1 hour

I dare to doubt whether the sweet Danube River waves are actually a purely Bavarian invention, but since this majestic river is a large part of the Free State, the recipe for this delicious cake must certainly find its way into these pages.
It is unknown how the waves got their name. With lots of imagination, the two superimposed floors of dough – one is somehow reminded of flowing water in its sandy bed, along with the cherries as river pebbles bright, the other layer of cake dark as a river bed.
In some areas of Germany, the Danube wave is called "Snow-white cake," precisely because it is "white as snow, red as blood, and black as ebony."

INGREDIENTS

FOR THE DOUGH

1/2 lb butter at room temperature
1 cup sugar
6 eggs
1 pinch salt
3 1/5 cups flour
2 tsp baking powder
3 Tb milk
3 Tb cocoa powder
1 1/2 lbs cherries from the glass, drained

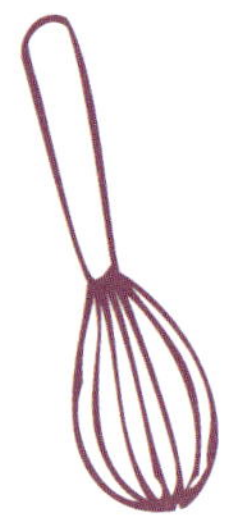

FOR THE CREAM

1 sachet vanilla pudding powder (see pg. 24)
2 cups milk
1/3 cup powdered sugar
1/2 lb butter at room temperature

IN ADDITION 1 small, deep baking pan, butter to grease the plate, 10 1/2 oz dark couverture

METHOD

Preheat the oven to 400°F.
Beat sugar with butter in a bowl. Gradually stir in eggs. Then add salt, flour and baking powder and form a tough sponge. Spread half of the dough evenly on a greased baking tray. Add to the rest of the dough in the bowl milk and cocoa powder and stir until dough is a dark color. The dough should be like pancakes – light and smooth. Spread cherries evenly on the

Milch und Kakaopulver geben und unterrühren, sodass ein dunkler Rührteig entsteht. Den Teig löffelweise auf den hellen Teig geben und dann glatt verstreichen. Schattenmorellen gleichmäßig darauf verteilen und das Ganze ca. 20–30 Minuten im Ofen backen. Stäbchenprobe machen! Auskühlen lassen.
Für die Creme das Puddingpulver – nach Packungsanweisung – mit jeweils 2–3 EL von der Ursprungsmenge Milch und dem Puderzucker glatt verrühren. Den Rest der Milch in einen Topf geben und aufkochen lassen. Pudding einrühren und noch eine Minute köcheln lassen. Dann den Rest des Puderzuckers unterrühren. Vom Herd nehmen und komplett auskühlen lassen. Butter für die Creme weich rühren und unter den erkalteten Pudding mengen.
Die Puddingcreme auf der Kuchenoberfläche verteilen und glatt streichen.
Kuvertüre im Wasserbad erhitzen und gleichmäßig über der Creme verteilen. Leicht abkühlen lassen und zum Abschluss mit der Gabel oder einem gezackten Teigkratzer zusätzliche »Wellen« durch die Kuvertüre ziehen.

Tipp *Donauwellen schmecken am besten kühl, also vor dem Verzehr – am besten über Nacht – im Kühlschrank kalt stellen.*

dough and bake for 20–30 minutes in the oven. Skewer test. Allow to cool off.
For the cream mix pudding powder – according to package directions – with 2–3 Tb of milk and the powdered sugar and stir until smooth. Pour the rest of the milk in a pot and boil. Stir in pudding and let it simmer for another minute. Then stir in the rest of the icing sugar. Remove from heat and cool completely. Softly stir in butter to the cream and mix in the cooled pudding.
Distribute the pudding cream on the surface of the cake smoothly.
Heat the chocolate in a bain-marie and spread evenly over the cream. Cool slightly, to conclude using the fork or a serrated pastry scraper pull additional "waves" through the chocolate.

Tips & Hints *Danube waves taste best cool, so before eating – best overnight – refrigerate.*

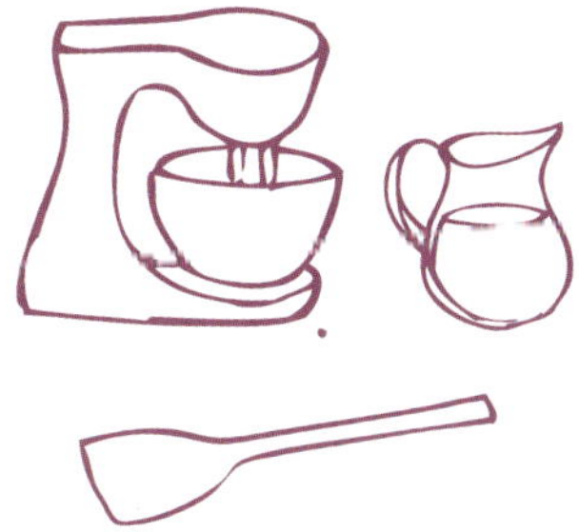

HEFEZOPF

Zubereitungszeit inkl. Gehzeiten für den Teig 1 Stunde 45 Minuten + Backzeit ca. 25–30 Minuten

ZUTATEN

FÜR DEN VORTEIG

20 g frische Hefe, zimmerwarm
2–3 EL lauwarme Milch
1 Prise Zucker
1–2 EL Mehl

FÜR DEN TEIG

500 g Mehl
Abrieb von 1/2 unbehandelten Zitrone
3 EL Zucker
1/8 l lauwarme Milch
2 Eier, zimmerwarm
nach Belieben 3–4 EL Rosinen, über Nacht in Rum oder Orangensaft eingeweicht
60 g Butter, zimmerwarm
1 Prise Salz

AUSSERDEM Backblech, Backpapier, ca. 50 g zerlassene Butter zum Bestreichen des Zopfes

ZUBEREITUNG

Hefe in eine kleine Schüssel bröckeln. Lauwarme Milch, 1 Prise Zucker und Mehl zugeben und mit der Hefe glatt verrühren. Abgedeckt an einem warmen, nicht zugigen Ort ca. 15 Minuten gehen lassen.
Mehl in eine große Schüssel sieben – oben eine Mulde eindrücken. Die aufgegangene Hefe in die Mulde geben und mit etwas Mehl bestäuben. Zitronenabrieb, Zucker, Milch und die Eier zugeben und alles locker miteinander verkneten. Wenn Sie möchten, können Sie nun die über Nacht eingeweichten und abgetropften Rosinen unterkneten (das ist reine Geschmackssache, der Zopf ist auch pur ein Genuss).
Zum Schluss Butter und Salz zugeben und alles zusammen zu einem geschmeidigen Teig kneten, der sich gut von der Schüssel löst. Mit einem Geschirrtuch abdecken und 1 Stunde an einem warmen, nicht zugigen Ort gehen lassen.
Backofen auf 200 Grad vorheizen.
Den aufgegangenen Teig noch einmal ordentlich durchkneten und dann in 3 gleich große Stücke teilen. Jedes Stück zu einem ca. 30 cm langen Strang rollen und daraus einen Zopf flechten.

BRAIDED BREAD

Preparation time including resting time for the dough 1 hour 45 minutes + baking time 25–30 minutes

INGREDIENTS

FOR THE YEAST STARTER

7/10 oz fresh yeast at room temperature
2–3 Tb lukewarm milk
1 pinch sugar
1–2 Tb flour

FOR THE DOUGH

4 cups flour
grated rind of 1/2 untreated lemon
3 Tb sugar
1/2 cup lukewarm milk
2 eggs at room temperature
3–4 Tb raisins, soaked overnight in rum or orange juice, to taste
4 Tb butter at room temperature
1 pinch salt

IN ADDITION baking sheet, baking paper, approx. 3 1/2 Tb melted butter for brushing the braid

METHOD

Crumble yeast in a small bowl. Stir lukewarm milk, 1 pinch of sugar and flour smoothly with the yeast. Leave in a warm, draft-free place for 15 minutes.
Sift flour in a large bowl and make a hollow in the middle. Crumble or sprinkle the yeast starter in the cavity and sprinkle with some flour. Knead the grated rind of lemon, sugar, milk and eggs loosely together. If you want, you can now add the drained raisins (which is purely a matter of taste).
Finally add butter and salt. Knead to a smooth dough that dissolves well by the bowl. Cover with a tea towel and leave for 1 hour in a warm, draft-free place.
Preheat the oven to 400°F.
The risen dough once properly kneaded can then be divided into 3 equal pieces. Roll each piece to an approximately 12 inches long strand and make a plait weave for a braid.
Place on the prepared baking sheet and leave again covered for 30 minutes.
Bake the bread in the oven for about 25–30 minutes until golden brown. Remove from the oven and while still warm coat

Auf das vorbereitete Backblech legen und nochmals abgedeckt 30 Minuten gehen lassen.
Im Ofen in ca. 25–30 Minuten goldbraun backen. Aus dem Ofen nehmen und noch warm mit zerlassener Butter bestreichen.
Hefezopf schmeckt am besten frisch aus dem Ofen und noch warm mit Butter und Marmelade bestrichen.

Tipps

- *Sie können den noch lauwarmen Hefezopf auch mit Mandelstiften und Hagelzucker garnieren.*
- *Hefezopf lässt sich gut einfrieren und im Backofen bei niedriger Temperatur wieder sanft aufwärmen.*

with melted butter. Braided bread tastes best fresh from the oven and still warm with butter and jam.

Tips & Hints

- *If you prefer, you can, while it is still somewhat warm, garnish the braided bread with almond splitters and coarse sugar.*
- *Braided bread freezes well; gently reheat again in the oven at a low temperature.*

OBERBAYERISCHER QUARKKUCHEN

Zubereitungszeit inkl. Backzeit ca. 2 Stunden

Das Rezept stammt von einer Bäuerin aus dem bayerischen Voralpenland. Dieser Quarkkuchen hat es in sich, fangen Sie also erst gar nicht an mit Kalorienzählen – lassen Sie ihn sich einfach auf der Zunge zergehen; er ist jede Sünde wert.

ZUTATEN

FÜR DEN TEIG

180 g kalte Butter
150 g Zucker
1 Ei, direkt aus dem Kühlschrank
270 g Mehl
2 TL Backpulver

FÜR DIE FÜLLUNG

500 g Sahne
4 Eier
150 g Zucker
4 TL (2 Pck.) Vanillezucker
Abrieb von 1 unbehandelten Zitrone
1 Pck. Vanillepuddingpulver
750 g Magerquark, 20% Fett i. Tr.

AUSSERDEM 1 Springform, 26 cm Durchmesser, etwas Butter und Semmelbrösel zum Einfetten und Ausstäuben der Form, Nudelholz

ZUBEREITUNG

Aus den Zutaten für den Teig eine feste Teigkugel kneten. Mit dem Nudelholz gleichmäßig ausrollen und in die vorbereitete Form geben. Den Teig an den Rändern der Form hochziehen. Im Kühlschrank zwischenlagern.
Für die Füllung Sahne steif schlagen und beiseitestellen.
Backofen auf 150 Grad vorheizen.
Eier, Zucker und Vanillezucker schaumig schlagen. Dann Zitronenabrieb, Vanillepuddingpulver und Quark unterrühren, sodass eine cremige Masse entsteht. Zum Schluss die steife Sahne zugeben und alles verrühren.
Springform aus dem Kühlschrank nehmen und die Quarkmasse auf den Teig geben. Den Kuchen ca. 90 Minuten im Ofen backen, bis der Teigrand eine goldgelbe Farbe angenommen hat.

UPPER-BAVARIAN CHEESECAKE

Preparation time including baking time approx. 2 hours

The recipe comes from a farmer's wife from the Bavarian Alps. This cheesecake has it all, so don't start counting calories – it is simply a-melt-in-your-mouth sin and worth every calorie.

INGREDIENTS

FOR THE DOUGH

12 Tb cold butter
2/3 cup sugar
1 egg, straight from the fridge
2 cups flour
2 tsp baking powder

FOR THE FILLING

2 cups cream
4 eggs
2/3 cup sugar
4 tsp (2 sachets) vanilla sugar
grated rind of 1 untreated lemon
1 sachet vanilla pudding powder (see pg. 24)
3 cups low-fat curd cheese

IN ADDITION 1 spring form pan, 10 inches in diameter, some butter and breadcrumbs to grease and dust the pan, rolling pin

METHOD

Knead the ingredients for the dough into a solid ball of dough. Evenly roll out with rolling pin and place in the prepared pan. Pull the dough around the edges of the pan. Store in the refrigerator.
For the filling, whip cream and set aside.
Preheat the oven to 300°F.
Beat eggs, sugar and vanilla sugar until foamy. Then stir the grated lemon rind, vanilla pudding powder and curd cheese together, so a creamy mixture is obtained. Finally add the stiff cream and stir everything together.
Remove spring form pan from the refrigerator and spread the curd cheese mixture all over the dough. Bake the cake for about 90 minutes in the oven until the edge of the dough becomes a golden color.

Vorsichtig aus dem Ofen holen – die Füllung wackelt immer noch bedenklich, aber das ist ein gutes Zeichen! – und den Kuchen komplett abkühlen lassen, bevor Sie ihn anschneiden und servieren. Wird der Quarkkuchen zu früh, also noch warm, angeschnitten, zerfällt die fragile Füllung und der schöne Kuchen ist dahin!

Remove carefully from the oven – the filling will still jiggle, but that is a good sign – leave the cake to completely cool before you cut it and serve. If the cheesecake is cut while still warm, the fragile filling will collapse and the beautiful cake is destroyed.

OBSTSTREUSEL

Ergibt 1 Blech, also ca. 12 große oder 24 kleine Stücke
Zubereitungszeit inkl. Backzeit ca. 1 Stunde

ZUTATEN

500 g Butter, zimmerwarm
750 g Mehl
2 TL (1 Pck.) Vanillezucker
300 g Vollrohrzucker
Abrieb von 1 unbehandelten Zitrone
1 TL Anissamen, grob gemörsert
1 Prise Salz
ca. 1 kg gewaschenes und vorbereitetes Obst, z. B. Kirschen, Aprikosen oder Zwetschgen (geviertelt), Stachelbeeren, Johannisbeeren usw.
100 g Mandelblättchen

AUSSERDEM 1 tiefes Backblech, Knethaken, etwas Butter und Mehl zum Einfetten und Bestäuben des Blechs

ZUBEREITUNG

Butter, Mehl, Vanillezucker, Vollrohrzucker, Zitronenabrieb, Anis und Salz in eine Schüssel geben und mit Knethaken zunächst grob vermengen. Dann die Hände zu Hilfe nehmen und den Teig zu einer groben Streuselmasse fertig kneten.
Backofen auf 200 Grad vorheizen.
Zwei Drittel der Streuselmasse auf dem ausreichend eingefetteten und bemehlten Backblech verteilen und mit den Händen zu einem festen Boden drücken. Obst gleichmäßig auf dem Teigboden verteilen.
Mandelblättchen unter das restliche Drittel des Streuselteigs mischen und alles gleichmäßig über das Obst geben. Den Obststreusel auf unterster Schiene im Backofen ca. 40 Minuten goldbraun backen. Vor dem Anschneiden gut auskühlen lassen.

Tipp *Der Vollrohrzucker gibt dem Kuchen eine leichte Karamellnote. Sie können Ihren Obststreusel aber auch mit herkömmlichem Zucker backen.*

FRUIT CRUMBLE

Yields 1 sheet, so about 12 large or 24 small pieces
Preparation time including baking time approx. 1 hour

INGREDIENTS

1 lb butter at room temperature
6 cups flour
2 tsp (1 sachet) vanilla sugar
1 1/2 cups whole cane sugar
grated rind of 1 untreated lemon
1 tsp Anis seeds, coarsely ground
1 pinch salt
7 cups washed and prepared fruit, such as cherries, apricots or plums (quartered), gooseberries, currants, etc.
1/2 cup almond flakes

IN ADDITION 1 deep baking pan, dough hook, some butter and flour for greasing and dusting of sheet metal

METHOD

Mix butter, flour, vanilla sugar, whole cane sugar, grated lemon peel, salt in a bowl and coarsely mix with dough hooks first. Then use your hands to knead the dough making sure it is a dry and crumbly consistency.
Preheat the oven to 400°F.
Distribute two thirds of the dough in the sufficiently greased and floured baking sheet and press with your hands to a solid base. Evenly spread the fruit on the dough.
Blend almonds with the remaining one third of the crumble dough and spread everything evenly over the fruit. Place it on the bottom rail in the oven for about 40 minutes until the fruit crumble is browned. Let it cool well before cutting.

Tips & Hints *The whole cane sugar gives the cake a light hint of caramel. You can also bake your fruit crumble using conventional sugar.*

OSTERBROT

Ergibt 1 Laib
Zubereitungszeit inkl. Backzeit 1 Stunde +
Gehzeit 1,5 Stunden

Dem Osterbrot, auch Osterfladen genannt, wird im katholischen Bayern eine große Bedeutung zugemessen, symbolisiert es doch, zusammen mit anderen traditionell ausgewählten Lebensmitteln, das Ende der Fastenzeit. Am Ostersonntag, teilweise auch schon am Karfreitag, bringen die Menschen Körbe mit Essbarem in ihre Kirchen, um diese am Altar segnen zu lassen. Osterlämmer aus Biskuitteig, geräuchertes Fleisch, Salz und Meerrettich; das alles soll an das bittere Leiden Jesu Christi am Kreuz erinnern. Gefärbte Eier bezeugen die Fruchtbarkeit der Erde und lassen auf ein gutes Erntejahr hoffen.
Dem Osterbrot fällt die besondere Bedeutung der Auferstehung zu. In manchen Gegenden Bayerns werden Safranfäden mit in den Teig gegeben. Die gelbe Färbung soll die aufgehende Sonne symbolisieren, die Morgenröte nach einer dunklen Nacht.

ZUTATEN

FÜR DEN VORTEIG

20 g frische Hefe
2 EL lauwarmes Wasser
1 Prise Zucker
1 EL Mehl

FÜR DEN TEIG

ca. 300 g Mehl
50 g Butter, zimmerwarm
40 g Zucker
2 TL (1 Pck.) Vanillezucker
1/8 l Milch, zimmerwarm
Abrieb von 1 unbehandelten Zitrone
2 Eier, zimmerwarm
1 Prise Salz
50 g Sultaninen
1 Eigelb zum Bestreichen
nach Belieben Hagelzucker zum Bestreuen

AUSSERDEM Backpapier, 1 Backblech, scharfes Messer oder Rasierklinge

EASTER BREAD

Yields 1 loaf
Preparation time including baking time 1 hour +
resting time 1.5 hours

The Easter bread, also known as Easter cakes, are of great importance to Catholic Bavaria, as it symbolizes the end of the fasting period, together with other selected traditional foods. On Easter Sunday, sometimes on Good Friday, people bring baskets with food into their churches to get it blessed at the altar. Anything from Easter lamb to sponge cakes, smoked meat, salt and horseradish; they all should remind us of the sufferings of Jesus Christ on the cross. Dyed eggs symbolize the fertility of the Earth and can bring luck for a good harvest for the year.
The importance of the resurrection is symbolized by the Easter bread. In some areas of Bavaria, saffron is added into the dough. The yellow color symbolizes the rising sun and the dawn after a dark night.

INGREDIENTS

FOR THE YEAST STARTER

7/10 oz fresh yeast
2 Tb lukewarm water
1 pinch sugar
1 Tb flour

FOR THE DOUGH

approx. 2 2/5 cups flour
3 Tb butter at room temperature
1 1/2 Tb sugar
2 tsp (1 sachet) vanilla sugar
1/2 cup milk at room temperature
grated rind of 1 untreated lemon
2 eggs at room temperature
1 pinch salt
1/3 cup golden sultanas
1 egg yolks for brushing
coarse sugar for sprinkling to taste

IN ADDITION baking paper, 1 baking sheet, sharp knife or razor blade

ZUBEREITUNG

Aus den Zutaten für den Vorteig in einer kleinen Schüssel das sogenannte »Dampferl« anrühren. Abdecken und an einem warmen, nicht zugigen Ort 30 Minuten gehen lassen.

Dann Mehl in eine große Schüssel sieben, eine Mulde in das Mehl drücken und den Vorteig einfüllen. Alle Zutaten der Reihenfolge nach zugeben und gut miteinander verkneten. Eier, Salz und Sultaninen bilden den Schluss. Ist der Teig zu klebrig, evtl. noch etwas Mehl unterkneten. Es sollte ein weicher, geschmeidiger, nicht klebriger Teigball entstehen. Mit einem Geschirrtuch abdecken und erneut 1 Stunde am selben Ort gehen lassen.

Backofen auf 200 Grad vorheizen.

Den Teig aus der Schüssel nehmen und ein letztes Mal gut durchkneten (evtl. noch mal etwas Mehl dazu, falls er immer noch ein bisschen klebt). Einen schönen runden Laib formen und auf das vorbereitete Backblech legen. Die Oberfläche des Teigs mit Eigelb einpinseln. Dann mit einem sehr scharfen Messer oder einer Rasierklinge rautenförmig einschneiden und, wenn Sie möchten, mit Hagelzucker bestreuen. Ca. 45 Minuten im Ofen goldbraun backen – nach 25 Minuten Backzeit die Hitze auf 150 Grad reduzieren.

Das fertige Osterbrot auskühlen lassen.

Tipps

- *Wie oben erwähnt, können Sie dem Teig ein paar Safranfäden zugeben, damit er sich schön gelb färbt. Ich persönlich finde, die beiden Eier, die den Teig leicht hellgelb färben, reichen vollkommen zur Farbgebung aus!*
- *Die Sultaninen können Sie natürlich weglassen; nicht jeder mag getrocknete Weinbeeren.*
- *Osterbrot schmeckt am besten lauwarm und dick mit Butter und Marmelade bestrichen. Aber auch mit zartem Schinken belegt, ist das Brot ein Gedicht.*
- *Fest in Frischhaltefolie gewickelt (zuvor das Brot wirklich komplett auskühlen lassen), hält sich das Osterbrot mehrere Tage lang.*

METHOD

Stir the ingredients for the yeast starter in a small bowl for the so-called "Dampferl." Cover and leave in a warm, draft-free place for 30 minutes.

Then sift the flour into a large bowl, forming a hollow in the flour and pour the dough. Add all ingredients in order after and knead well together. At the end add the eggs, salt and sultanas. If the dough is too sticky, knead in some extra flour. A soft, smooth but not sticky dough ball should form. Cover with a tea towel and again leave it for 1 hour at the same location.

Preheat the oven to 400°F.

Take the dough out of the bowl and knead one last time well (you may need to add some more flour if dough is still sticky). Make a nice round loaf shape and place on the prepared baking sheet. Brush the surface of the dough with the egg yolk. Then cut a diamond shape with a very sharp knife or a razor blade and, if you like, sprinkle with sugar. Bake 45 minutes in the oven until golden brown – after 25 minutes baking time, reduce heat to 300°F.

Allow to cool and the Easter bread is completed.

Tips & Hints

- *As mentioned above, you can add a few strands of saffron to the dough, so it turns a beautiful shade of yellow. Personally, I find the two eggs completely sufficient to provide a slightly pale yellowish color to the color scheme.*
- *You can, of course, omit the sultanas; not everyone likes dried grapes.*
- *Easter bread tastes best warm and with a thick layer of butter and jam. It is just as delicious served with sliced boiled ham.*
- *Tightly wrapped in plastic wrap (ensure bread is completely cooled), the Easter bread keeps for several days.*

PRINZREGENTENTORTE

Zubereitungszeit inkl. Backzeit ca. 2,5 Stunden + mindestens 12 Stunden Ruhezeit

Der Name dieser im doppelten Wortsinn »mächtigen« Torte – zählen Sie lieber nicht die Kalorien! – bezieht sich auf den Prinzregenten Luitpold, der als Nachfolger des sagenumwobenen Königs Ludwig II. bis zum Jahre 1912 das Königreich Bayern regierte. Im Original, von einem findigen Münchner Konditor zu Ehren des beliebten Monarchen erfunden, hatte die Prinzregententorte einst acht Tortenböden, welche die acht Regierungsbezirke Bayerns versinnbildlichen sollten. Sie ist also tatsächlich eine durch und durch bayerische und zudem auch noch königliche Kreation, auch wenn wir uns im folgenden Rezept, wie heutzutage in vielen Konditoreien üblich, auf sechs Böden beschränken.

ZUTATEN

FÜR DEN TEIG

250 g Butter, zimmerwarm
200 g Mehl
1 EL Speisestärke
1 TL Backpulver
1 Prise Salz
250 g Zucker
2 TL (1 Pck.) Vanillezucker
5 große Eier
3 Eigelb
3 Eiweiß, mit 1 Prise Salz mindestens 7 Minuten lang sehr steif geschlagen

FÜR DIE CREME

200 g dunkle Schokolade, 60% Kakaoanteil
200 g Butter, zimmerwarm
125 g Puderzucker
3 Eigelb
5 EL Weinbrand

FÜR DIE GLASUR

ca. 150 g Aprikosenmarmelade
200 g Zartbitterkuvertüre

AUSSERDEM Boden von 1 Springform, 26 cm Durchmesser, reichlich Butter zum Einfetten des Bodens, ausreichend Back- oder Butterbrotpapier

PRINCE REGENT'S CAKE

Preparation time including baking time approx. 2.5 hours + at least 12 hours rest period

The name of this cake is described as "rich" – better not to count the calories – and refers to the Prince Regent Luitpold of Bavaria, who ruled the Kingdom of Bavaria as a successor of the fabled King Ludwig II until 1912. Originally invented by a resourceful Munich-based confectioner, in honor of the popular monarch, the Prince Regent's cake once had eight cakes, which should symbolize the eight administrative districts of Bavaria. It can in fact be found throughout Bavaria in many pastry shops and is not only a thoroughly Bavarian but also royal creation.

INGREDIENTS

FOR THE DOUGH

1/2 lb butter at room temperature
1 3/5 cups flour
1 Tb starch
1 tsp baking soda
1 pinch salt
1 cup sugar
2 tsp (1 sachet) vanilla sugar
5 large eggs
3 egg yolks
3 very stiff egg whites, beaten with a pinch of salt at least 7 minutes

FOR THE CREAM

7 oz dark chocolate, 60% cocoa
1/2 lb butter at room temperature
1 cup powdered sugar
3 egg yolks
5 Tb brandy

FOR THE GLAZE

approx. 1/3 lb apricot jam
7 oz dark chocolate

IN ADDITION floor of 1 spring form pan, 10 inches in diameter, plenty of butter to grease the bottom, enough baking or greaseproof paper

ZUBEREITUNG

Zuerst den Backofen auf 200 Grad vorheizen, denn der Teig benötigt später die volle Hitze, um zu gelingen.
Die Butter für den Teig in Stückchen schneiden – dann lässt sie sich leichter verarbeiten – und in einer Schüssel cremig rühren. Mehl, Stärke und Backpulver in einer zweiten Schüssel miteinander vermengen und anschließend fein sieben. Nun, nach und nach, im Wechsel Salz, Zucker, Vanillezucker, die 5 Eier, 3 Eigelbe und das gesiebte Mehlgemisch unter die Buttercreme rühren, sodass eine luftige Teigmasse entsteht. Abschließend den Eischnee vorsichtig unterheben.
Den Boden der Springform gut mit Butter einfetten. Sie benötigen zum Backen nur den Boden der Form, nicht den Rand. Nun 3 EL Teig gleichmäßig auf dem eingefetteten Boden dünn verstreichen – allerdings nicht zu dünn, sonst bekommen Sie den fertigen Boden nicht mehr von der Form.
Den Rest des Teigs kühl stellen.
Den Boden im Backrohr ca. 8–10 Minuten goldgelb backen. Anschließend den Teigboden vorsichtig, falls nötig mit einem

METHOD

First preheat the oven to 400°F because the dough needs the full heat later.
Cut the butter for the dough into cubes – then it can be more easily mixed – and form a creamy mixture in a bowl. Mix starch, flour and baking powder in a second bowl together and then finely sift. Now, gradually, alternating, stir salt, sugar, vanilla sugar, 5 eggs, egg yolks and the sifted flour mixture into the butter cream, which creates an airy dough. Finally gently stir in the beaten egg whites.
Grease the bottom of the spring form pan with butter. You only need the bottom of the pan, not the edge. Now spread 3 Tb dough evenly and thinly on the bottom of the greased form – but not too thin, or you no longer get the finished floor off the pan.
Refrigerate the rest of the dough.
Bake the dough approximately 8–10 minutes in the oven until golden. Loosen the bottom of the dough gently, if necessary with a knife, and cool on a wire rack.

Messer, lösen und auf einem Kuchengitter auskühlen lassen. Normalerweise »flutscht« er von ganz alleine vom Springformboden.

Den Springformboden unter fließend kaltem Wasser abkühlen, dann erneut großzügig mit Butter einfetten und mit dem nächsten Teigboden genauso verfahren. Den restlichen Teig immer wieder kühl stellen. Insgesamt werden so 6 Böden gebacken.

Für die Schokoladencreme-Füllung die Bitterschokolade in Stückchen brechen und im Wasserbad schmelzen, dann zum Abkühlen beiseitestellen.

Während die Schokolade abkühlt, wird die weiche, in Stückchen geschnittene Butter mit dem Puderzucker und den Eigelben in einer separaten Schüssel schaumig gerührt. Zum Abschluss den Weinbrand und die abgekühlte Schokolade unterrühren.

Nun die Tortenböden gleichmäßig mit der Creme bestreichen und auf die Tortenplatte schichten, der oberste Boden bleibt frei.

Die Aprikosenmarmelade in einen kleinen Topf geben und erhitzen. Mit einem Pinsel gleichmäßig auf der Torte verteilen. Dann die Kuvertüre im Wasserbad erhitzen und noch warm auf die gesamte Torte geben und glatt streichen.

Damit sich die Schichten gut verbinden, muss die Prinzregententorte an einem kühlen Ort 12 Stunden lang – am besten über Nacht zugedeckt im Kühlschrank – ruhen.

Tipps

- *Ich leihe mir bei meinen Nachbarinnen im Haus so viele Springformen gleicher Größe wie möglich. So kann ich schneller arbeiten. Als Dankeschön gibt es dann für jede ein Stück Torte.*
- *Sollte sich der fertige Teigboden nach dem Backen nicht von der Form lösen, hilft ein bewährter alter Haushaltstrick: Einfach einen Spüllappen mit kaltem Wasser tränken und vor dem Stürzen ein paar Minuten lang von unten an den heißen Springformboden pressen.*
- *Sie können die einzelnen Böden, bevor Sie sie mit der Schokoladencreme bestreichen, zusätzlich mit Aprikosenmarmelade bepinseln, das macht die Torte noch saftiger – erhitzen Sie dazu 150 g mehr Marmelade als oben angegeben.*

Generously grease the spring form pan bottom again with butter and cover again until the base is not visible. Always again refrigerate the remaining batter. As a whole, 6 layers are baked.

For the chocolate cream filling melt broken up pieces of chocolate in a bain-marie, then leave it to cool down.

While the chocolate cools, mix the soft, cut up pieces of butter with the powdered sugar and the egg yolks in a separate bowl until foamy. Finally stir in the brandy and the cooled chocolate.

Now drizzle the cream evenly over the cake bottoms and layer on the cake plate; the top floor remains free.

Place the apricot jam in a small saucepan and heat (so the jam is liquid and can be easily used). Spread evenly on the top of the cake with a brush.

Then heat the chocolate in a bain-marie and then cover the entire pie still warm with this chocolate.

To ensure that the layers combine well, leave the Prince Regent's cake in a cool place to rest for 12 hours – best when covered overnight in the fridge.

Tips & Hints

- *I borrowed so many spring form pans as close to same size as possible from my neighbours, so I could work faster. As a thank you, I offered them a piece of cake.*
- *Should the finished dough bottom not loosen and detach after the baking stage, here is an old proven domestic trick: simply soak a dish cloth with cold water and press it against the bottom for a few minutes before turning upside down and releasing the cake from the bottom of the spring form pan.*
- *Before you coat them with the chocolate cream, you can also brush the individual bottoms with apricot jam, which makes the pie even juicier – heat 1/3 lb more of jam than specified above.*

QUARKSTREUSEL

Ergibt 1 Blech, ca. 12 Stücke
Zubereitungszeit ca. 30 Minuten + Gehzeiten für den Teig insgesamt 1 Stunde + Backzeit ca. 30–40 Minuten

Dieses Rezept stammt von der gleichen Bäuerin wie der Oberbayerische Quarkkuchen auf einer der vorherigen Seiten. Und genau wie ihr Quarkkuchen schmeckt auch dieser Blechkuchen sensationell! Lassen Sie sich von der Mengenangabe des Topfens, also des Quarks, nicht beirren: Hier hat alles seine Richtigkeit!

ZUTATEN

FÜR DEN VORTEIG

20 g frische Hefe
1 EL Mehl
1–2 EL lauwarmes Wasser
1 Prise Salz

FÜR DEN TEIG

300 g Mehl
80 g Butter, zimmerwarm
60 g Zucker
1/8 l lauwarme Milch
1 Ei, zimmerwarm
Abrieb von 1 unbehandelten Zitrone
1 Prise Salz

FÜR DIE FÜLLUNG

80 g Butter, zimmerwarm
150 g Zucker
2 TL (1 Pck.) Vanillezucker
3 Eier
1 EL Stärkemehl
1 kg Quark, 40% Fett i. Tr.
20 ml Rum
Saft von 1 Zitrone

FÜR DIE STREUSEL

350 g Mehl
100 g Zucker
200 g Butter, zimmerwarm
1/2 TL Zimtpulver
1 Prise Salz

AUSSERDEM Nudelholz, etwas Mehl für die Arbeitsfläche, Backpapier, 1 tiefes Backblech

CURD CHEESE CRUMBLE

Yields 1 plate, approx. 12 pieces
Preparation time 30 minutes + resting time for the dough total 1 hour + baking time 30–40 minutes

This recipe comes from the same farmer that created the cheesecake on one of the previous pages. And just like their cheesecake, also this sheet cake tastes sensational. Here the quantities are stated for a reason, and it is important that they are measured correctly, especially the curd cheese.

INGREDIENTS

FOR THE YEAST STARTER

7/10 oz fresh yeast
1 Tb flour
1–2 Tb lukewarm water
1 pinch salt

FOR THE DOUGH

2 2/5 cups flour
5 1/2 Tb butter at room temperature
5 Tb sugar
1/2 cup lukewarm milk
1 egg at room temperature
grated rind of 1 untreated lemon
1 pinch salt

FOR THE FILLING

5 1/2 Tb butter at room temperature
1/4 cup sugar
2 tsp (1 sachet) vanilla sugar
3 eggs
1 Tb starch flour
4 cups curd cheese
4 tsp rum
juice of 1 lemon

FOR THE CRUMBLE

2 4/5 cups flour
1/2 cup sugar
14 Tb butter at room temperature
1/2 tsp cinnamon powder
1 pinch salt

IN ADDITION rolling pin, some flour for the work surface, baking paper, 1 deep baking pan

ZUBEREITUNG

Alle Zutaten für den Vorteig, das sogenannte »Dampferl«, in eine kleine Schüssel geben und glatt verrühren. Zudecken und an einem warmen, nicht zugigen Ort ca. 30 Minuten gehen lassen.

Dann das Mehl in eine große Schüssel geben, eine Mulde in den Mehlberg drücken und die aufgegangene Hefe einfüllen. Die restlichen Zutaten für den Teig nach und nach zugeben und mit den Knethaken des Handrührgeräts verkneten, bis sich der Teig leicht von der Schüssel löst. Eventuell noch etwas Mehl zugeben, wenn der Teig zu sehr klebt. Zudecken und erneut am selben Ort 30 Minuten gehen lassen.

Währenddessen in einer separaten Schüssel für die Füllung Butter mit Zucker und Vanillezucker schaumig schlagen. Dann ein Ei nach dem anderen unterrühren. Stärkemehl zugeben und unterrühren. Zum Schluss mit Quark, Rum und Zitronensaft glatt rühren.

Den Backofen auf 200 Grad vorheizen.

Den Teig auf einer leicht bemehlten Arbeitsfläche ausrollen und dann auf das vorbereitete Backblech legen. Den Teig dabei an den Rändern des Blechs etwas hochziehen. Quarkmasse gleichmäßig einfüllen und glatt streichen.

Die Zutaten für die Streusel mit den Händen zu einem krümeligen Teig verarbeiten. Die Streusel dick auf dem Quark verteilen. 30–40 Minuten im Ofen goldgelb backen. Vor dem Anschneiden ganz auskühlen lassen.

Tipp *Statt der Quarkfüllung eignet sich auch ein Belag mit frischen Früchten, wie Zwetschgen oder Aprikosen.*

METHOD

Add all the ingredients for the yeast starter in a small bowl and stir smoothly. Cover and leave in a warm, draft-free place for 30 minutes.

Then add the flour in a large bowl, make a hollow in the flour and enter the yeast starter into the hole. Gradually add the remaining ingredients for the dough and knead the dough using a hand mixer, until it raises easily from the bowl. Add more flour if the dough is too sticky. Cover and leave again in the same place for 30 minutes.

Meanwhile fill a separate bowl with sugar, vanilla sugar and butter and beat until fluffy. Then, stir in the eggs one after another. Stir in starch flour. Conclude by smoothly stirring in the curd cheese, rum and lemon juice.

Preheat oven to 400°F.

Roll out the dough on a lightly floured work surface and then put it on the prepared baking sheet. Pull up the dough at the edges of the plate. Evenly fill and smoothly paint.

Mix the ingredients for the crumble with your hands to make a crumbly dough. Sprinkle the dough on the curd cheese in a thick layer. Bake for 30–40 minutes in the oven until golden. Allow to completely cool before cutting.

Tips & Hints *Instead of the curd cheese filling you can also use a surface with fresh fruit, such as plums or apricots.*

ROTE-BETE-SCHOKOLADEN-KUCHEN VOM BLECH

Ergibt 1 Blech, ca. 12 sehr große oder 24 kleinere Stücke
Zubereitungszeit inkl. Backzeit ca. 1 Stunde 20 Minuten

Lassen Sie sich nicht von der Roten Bete abschrecken! Die dunkelrote Knolle, deren Saft umgangssprachlich auch »Ochsenblut« genannt wird, macht diesen Schokoladenkuchen unvergleichlich saftig und vollmundig. Auch die Mengenangaben sind auf den ersten Blick etwas gewöhnungsbedürftig, aber dadurch bekommt der Kuchen eine schön dichte Struktur, ähnlich einer Sachertorte. Dem Vergleich mit dieser berühmten Wiener Spezialität hält übrigens unser Rote-Bete-Schokokuchen locker stand. Aber das ist meine ganz persönliche Meinung. Das Rezept stammt aus dem Münchner Gartensalon im schönen Stadtteil Schwabing, einem Café, in dem ich regelmäßig als Köchin am Herd stehe.

ZUTATEN

400 g Mehl
4 TL Backpulver
400 g Muscovadozucker
6 Eier
400 g zerlassene Butter, leicht abgekühlt
500 g weich gekochte Rote Bete, geschält, in feine Stücke geschnitten und anschließend püriert (dazu eignet sich sehr gut bereits vorgekochte und in Vakuum verschweißte Rote Bete aus dem Supermarkt)
400 g dunkle Schokolade, 70% Kakaoanteil, im Wasserbad geschmolzen und leicht abgekühlt
Mark von 1 Vanilleschote
4 EL Kakaopulver

AUSSERDEM 1 tiefes Backblech, Butter und Mehl zum Einfetten und Ausstäuben des Blechs, 200 g Zartbitterkuvertüre

ZUBEREITUNG

Backofen auf 175 Grad vorheizen.
Alle Zutaten für den Teig nach und nach miteinander verrühren, sodass ein dunkler Rührteig entsteht. Den Teig in das vorbereitete Backblech füllen und im Ofen ca. 40 Minuten backen. Stäbchenprobe machen! Auskühlen lassen.
Kuvertüre im Wasserbad erhitzen und auf der Oberfläche des Kuchens hauchdünn verstreichen.

RED BEETROOT CHOCOLATE CAKE FROM THE TIN

Yields 1 sheet, about 12 large or 24 small pieces
Preparation time including baking time approx. 1 hour 20 minutes

Don't let the red beet deter you from this heavenly delight. The dark bulb, whose juice is colloquially called "ox blood," makes this chocolate cake incomparably juicy and full-bodied. Also the quantities are really something at first glance, but this gives the cake a beautiful dense structure similar to a "Sacher" cake. Our red beetroot chocolate cake can be loosely compared to this famous Viennese specialty. But that's my personal opinion. The recipe comes from the Munich-based garden set in the beautiful district of Schwabing, a café in which I regularly work as a cook.

INGREDIENTS

4 1/5 cups flour
4 tsp baking powder
2 cups muscovado sugar
6 eggs
2 cups melted butter, slightly cooled
18 oz soft boiled beetroot, peeled, cut into fine pieces and then mashed (already pre-cooked and canned beetroot from the supermarket also works well)
1 1/2 cups dark chocolate, 70% cocoa content, melted in a water bath and slightly cooled
pulp from 1 vanilla bean
4 Tb cocoa powder

IN ADDITION 1 deep baking pan, butter and flour to grease and dust out the plate, 7 oz dark couverture

METHOD

Preheat the oven to 350°F.
Mix all the ingredients for the dough together, creating a dark sponge dough. Pour the mixture into the prepared baking tray and bake in the oven for about 40 minutes. Skewer test. Allow to cool off.
Melt chocolate in a bain-marie and spread a very thin layer on the surface of the cake.

Tipps

- *Sie können dieses Rezept auch für eine Springform mit 30 cm Durchmesser verwenden.*
- *Der Kuchen ist wirklich sehr schokoladig, sodass Sie auf die Kuvertüre auch verzichten können.*

Tips & Hints

- *You can also use this recipe using a spring form pan with a diameter of 12 inches.*
- *The cake is really very chocolaty, so you can also leave out the couverture.*

ZITRONENKUCHEN FÜR KLEINE BACKFORMEN

Zubereitungszeit 15 Minuten + Backzeit ca. 45 Minuten

Dieser Zitronenkuchen ist aus der Not heraus geboren: Ursprünglich wurde mir nachstehendes Rezept als »weltbestes Zitronenplätzchenrezept« zugetragen, doch als ich mich daranmachte, den Teig zuzubereiten, stellte ich fest, dass die Konsistenz eher mit einem Rührkuchenteig zu vergleichen war. Also kramte ich meine kleinste Kuchenform aus dem Schrank – et voilà!

ZUTATEN

100 g Butter, zimmerwarm
100 g Zucker
4 Eigelb, zimmerwarm
Saft und Abrieb von 1 unbehandelten Zitrone
150 g Mehl
50 g Stärke
1/2 TL Backpulver
30–50 g Zitronat, fein gehackt

AUSSERDEM 1 kleine Backform, z. B. Kastenbackform mit 20 cm Länge oder Springform mit 18 cm Durchmesser, Butter zum Einfetten und Mehl zum Ausstäuben der Form, 6 EL Puderzucker und Saft von 2 Zitronen für die Glasur, nach Belieben Puderzucker zum Bestäuben

ZUBEREITUNG

Backofen auf 180 Grad vorheizen.
Butter, Zucker und Eigelbe in einer Schüssel schaumig schlagen. Zitronensaft und fein geriebene Zitronenschale unterrühren. Mehl mit Stärke und Backpulver vermengen und in die Schaummasse sieben. Gut miteinander verrühren. Zum Schluss das fein gehackte Zitronat untermischen.
Minibackform gut mit Butter einfetten und anschließend mit Mehl ausstäuben. Den Teig gleichmäßig darin verstreichen. Den Kuchen ca. 45 Minuten goldgelb backen. Stäbchenprobe machen!
Für die Glasur Puderzucker und Zitronensaft miteinander vermengen und über den noch lauwarmen Kuchen geben, sodass ein Teil der Glasur in den Zitronenkuchen einziehen kann – das macht ihn schön saftig. Wenn Sie mögen, können Sie zum Abschluss noch etwas Puderzucker über den Kuchen stäuben.

LEMON CAKE FOR SMALL TINS

Preparation time 15 minutes + baking time 45 minutes

This lemon cake was born out of necessity: originally the following recipe was known as the "world's best lemon cookie recipe," but as for me, to prepare the dough, I noted that the consistency was rather similar to stirring a cake batter. So I dug around my closet looking for my smallest cake tin – et voilà!

INGREDIENTS

7 Tb butter at room temperature
1/2 cup sugar
4 egg yolks at room temperature
juice and grated rind of 1 untreated lemon
1 1/5 cups flour
approx. 1/2 cup starch
1/2 tsp baking powder
1–2 oz candied lemon peel, finely chopped

IN ADDITION 1 small baking pan, for example a box pan 8 inches length or spring form pan with 7 inches in diameter, butter to grease and flour to dust the pan, 6 Tb powdered sugar and juice of 2 lemons for the glaze, powdered sugar for dusting to taste

METHOD

Preheat the oven to 350°F.
Beat butter, sugar and egg yolks in a bowl until foamy. Stir in lemon juice and finely grated lemon zest. Mix flour with starch and baking soda and sift into the foamy consistency already made. Mix well together. Finally mix in the chopped candied lemon peel.
Grease mini baking pan well with butter and then with flour dust the surface. Spread the batter evenly on it. Bake the cake for about 45 minutes until golden. Skewer test.
For the glaze, mix powdered sugar and lemon juice together and pour over the still lukewarm cake, so that a part of the glaze can soak into the lemon cake – which makes it juicy. If you like, you can dust some powdered sugar over the cake at the end.

ZWETSCHGENDATSCHI

Zubereitungszeit ca. 20 Minuten + insgesamt ca. 1 Stunde 20 Minuten Ruhezeit für den Hefeteig + 30–40 Minuten Backzeit

Ein bayerischer Spätsommer ohne Zwetschgendatschi ist für uns Ureinwohner schlichtweg undenkbar. Die Kaffeetafel wird, wenn es das Wetter zulässt, draußen im Schatten gedeckt. Wespen lassen sich summend und halb wahnsinnig vor Begierde auf den süß-klebrigen Früchten nieder und der Duft von frisch aufgebrühtem Kaffee vermischt sich mit dem verheißungsvollen Geruch warmen Hefeteigs.

ZUTATEN

FÜR DEN VORTEIG

ca. 30 g frische Hefe
3 EL lauwarme Milch
1 Prise Zucker
ca. 1 EL Mehl

FÜR DEN TEIG

500 g Mehl
3 Eier
250 ml lauwarme Milch
1 EL zerlassene Butter
1 Prise Salz

FÜR DEN BELAG

2 kg Zwetschgen, gewaschen und entsteint
3 EL Zucker
1/2 TL Zimtpulver

AUSSERDEM Mehl zum Bestäuben der Arbeitsplatte, Backblech, Backpapier

ZUBEREITUNG

Die Hefe mit den Fingern zerbröseln und in eine Schüssel geben. Die restlichen Zutaten für den Vorteig zugeben und alles zusammen zu einer cremigen Masse rühren. Darauf achten, dass die Milch nicht zu heiß ist und dass Sie nicht zu viel Zucker verwenden, denn in beiden Fällen geht die Hefe nicht auf. Die Schüssel mit einem Küchentuch abdecken und dieses sogenannte »Dampferl« an einem warmen, nicht zugigen Ort ca. 15 Minuten gehen lassen.

PLUM SHEET CAKE

Preparation time approx. 20 minutes + resting time for leavened/yeast dough approx. 1 hour 20 minutes + 30–40 minutes baking time

A late summer without our beloved plum sheet cake is simply unimaginable for us Bavarians. Whenever the weather allows it, the coffee table is set outside in the shade. Wasps hum about loudly, overcome with a ravishing desire for the sticky-sweet fruits, while the fragrant aroma of freshly brewed coffee intertwines with the promising and comforting smell of leavened dough still radiating warm.

INGREDIENTS

FOR THE YEAST STARTER

approx. 1 oz yeast
3 Tb lukewarm milk
1 pinch sugar
approx. 1 Tb flour

FOR THE DOUGH

4 cups flour
3 eggs
1 cup lukewarm milk
1 Tb melted butter
1 pinch salt

FOR THE TOPPING

9 cups plums, washed and pitted
3 Tb sugar
1/2 tsp ground cinnamon

IN ADDITION flour for dusting the work surface, backing sheet, backing parchment

METHOD

Crumble the yeast into a bowl with your fingers. Add the remaining ingredients for the yeast starter and mix until creamy. Make sure the milk is not too hot and not to add too much sugar– in both cases the yeast will not rise. Cover the bowl with a kitchen towel and place this "Dampferl," as it is called in Bavaria, in a warm spot and let it rest for 15 minutes. Then add the remaining ingredients for the dough little by little; make sure the salt is added last (see pg. 12–13 for information on yeast dough); knead well, while repeatedly slamming the

Anschließend die restlichen Zutaten für den Teig der Reihe nach zum Vorteig geben – dabei darauf achten, dass das Salz tatsächlich den Schluss bildet (s. Informationen zum Hefeteig S. 13f.) – und alles gut miteinander verkneten. Den Teig während des Knetens mehrmals auf der Arbeitsfläche kräftig aufschlagen. Die Teigkugel erneut zugedeckt an einem warmen, nicht zugigen Ort 1 Stunde gehen lassen.
Den Backofen auf 200 Grad vorheizen. Den aufgegangenen Teig auf der bemehlten Arbeitsfläche ca. 1 cm dick ausrollen. Backblech mit Backpapier auslegen und den Teig darauflegen. Ein letztes Mal mit einem Küchentuch abdecken und 5 Minuten gehen lassen. Dann die Zwetschgen fächerförmig auf dem Teig anordnen. Die Früchte sollten sich dabei leicht überlappen. An den Seiten jeweils einen schmalen Rand aussparen.
Den Datschi ca. 30–40 Minuten backen, bis der Rand eine leicht bräunliche Färbung angenommen hat.
Den Zwetschgendatschi noch warm mit Zimt und Zucker bestreuen.

Tipps

- *Zu Zwetschgendatschi schmeckt am besten frisch aufgeschlagene Sahne.*
- *Vor dem Backen können Sie Mandelblättchen über die Zwetschgen streuen.*
- *Statt des Zimt-Zucker-Gemischs können Sie Ihren Zwetschgendatschi auch mit Butterstreuseln und Mandeln verfeinern. Für die Streusel 350 g Mehl, 200 g Zucker, 100 g Margarine und 100 g zimmerwarme Butter in eine Schüssel geben und mit den Fingern locker durchkneten, sodass kleine Klümpchen entstehen, die Sie dann gleichmäßig über den Zwetschgen verteilen. Zum Abschluss ca. 50 g Mandelblättchen über die Butterstreusel geben und dann im Ofen, wie oben angegeben, backen.*

dough onto the work surface. Place the dough in a bowl once more, letting it rest in a warm spot, where there is no draft, for one hour.
Preheat oven to 400°F. Place risen dough onto a floured work surface; roll it out to a 3/8-inch rectangle and then place it onto a baking sheet lined with baking parchment.
Cover with kitchen towel one last time and let rest for another 5 minutes. Then arrange the plums in a fan pattern on top of the dough; the plums should overlap. Leave a small edge on all sides. Bake the cake for approx. 30–40 minutes until the edges have turned slightly brown. Take the plum sheet cake out of the oven and sprinkle with cinnamon and sugar while still warm.

Tips & Hints

- *Freshly whipped cream is the best topping for traditional "Zwetschgendatschi."*
- *Before baking, you can sprinkle the "Zwetschgendatschi" with almond flakes.*
- *In place of a cinnamon-sugar mixture, you can top your "Zwetschgendatschi" with butter crumble and almonds. For the crumble, you will need 2 4/5 cups flour, 3/4 cup sugar, 1/2 cup margarine and 1/2 cup softened butter. Place all the ingredients into a bowl and knead lightly with your fingers, so that small clumps are formed. These are then evenly strewn over the plums. Before placing it in the oven, sprinkle 1/4 cup sliced almonds over the streusel and bake as directed above.*

Nachspeisen

Desserts

APFELKÜCHERL

Zubereitungszeit ca. 40 Minuten

Die Bayern bereiten ihre Süßigkeiten gerne mit viel Butterschmalz zu. Nun, in früheren Zeiten hatte man in den Vorratsschränken nicht allzu viele Zutaten lagernd, aber Schmalz und Mehl hatte fast jede Hausfrau ausreichend zur Verfügung. Und spätestens nach diesen herrlichen Apfelringen werden auch Sie damit versöhnt sein, versprochen!

ZUTATEN

5–6 säuerliche Äpfel, z. B. Cox Orange oder Elstar, geschält, mit einem Apfelstecher vom Kerngehäuse befreit und in ca. 1 cm dicke Ringe geschnitten
Saft von 1 Zitrone
200 g Mehl
3 Eier
ca. 1/8 l Milch
70 g Zucker
2 TL (1 Pck.) Vanillezucker
1 Prise Salz
nach Belieben 1 EL Rum

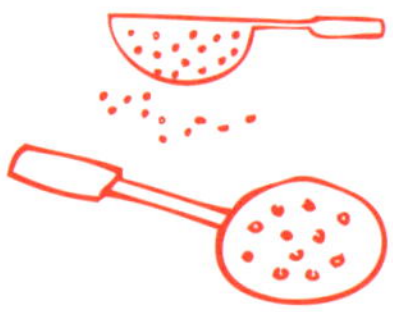

AUSSERDEM Zimt und Zucker zum Bestreuen, ausreichend Butterschmalz zum Ausbacken, Küchentuch zum Abtropfen

ZUBEREITUNG

Die Apfelringe mit Zitronensaft beträufeln, damit sie nicht braun werden. Mehl, Eier, Milch, Zucker, Vanillezucker und Salz in eine Schüssel geben und zu einem dicken Teig verrühren. Wenn Sie mögen, geben Sie noch einen Esslöffel Rum in den Teig. Den Teig zugedeckt ca. 10 Minuten ruhen lassen.
2 EL Butterschmalz in eine Pfanne geben und erhitzen. Nun nach und nach die Apfelringe durch den Teig ziehen und dann im heißen Fett auf beiden Seiten goldgelb ausbacken.
Wenn nötig, immer wieder neues Butterschmalz in die Pfanne geben, bis alle Ringe fertig gebacken sind. Die Apfelküchерl auf einem Küchentuch abtropfen lassen. Anschließend mit Zimt und Zucker bestreuen und noch warm servieren.

Tipp Reichen Sie zu Ihren Apfelkücherl halbfest geschlagene Sahne und/oder Vanilleeis.

APPLE RINGS

Preparation time approx. 40 minutes

As you have surely noticed during the chapter about the lard noodles and similar recipes, Bavarians like to use lots of clarified butter when preparing desserts. Back in the old days, pantry cabinets did not contain too many ingredients, especially in stock. Lard and flour, however, were sufficiently available to almost every housewife. And after having tried these wonderful Apple rings, you will surely also be more enthusiastic about it, promised.

INGREDIENTS

5–6 tart apples, e.g. Cox Orange or Elstar, cored and sliced into 3/8-inch rings
juice of 1 lemon
1 3/5 cups flour
3 eggs
approx. 1/2 cup milk
1/4 cup sugar
2 tsp (1 sachet) vanilla sugar
1 pinch salt
1 Tb rum to taste

IN ADDITION sugar and cinnamon for dusting, (enough) clarified butter for frying, paper towels for draining

METHOD

Sprinkle the apple rings with lemon juice to prevent them from discoloring. Place the flour, eggs, milk, sugar, vanilla sugar and salt into a bowl and mix until you have a thick batter. If you like, you can now also add a tablespoon of rum to the batter. Cover the bowl and let the batter rest for approximately 10 minutes.
Melt 3 1/2 Tb clarified butter in a pan. One at a time, dip the apple rings into the batter and then fry in hot fat until golden brown on both sides. If necessary, add more clarified butter to the pan until all apple rings are finished frying. Let the finished apple rings drain on a paper towel; sprinkle with cinnamon and sugar and serve while still warm.

Tips & Hints Serve apple rings with some whipped cream and/or vanilla ice cream.

APFELTIRAMISU

Zubereitungszeit ca. 30 Minuten + 1 Stunde Ruhezeit

ZUTATEN

750 g Äpfel, geschält, vom Kerngehäuse befreit und in kleine Stücke geschnitten
1 Zimtstange
1/4 unbehandelte Zitrone
ca. 1/8 l Apfelsaft
200 g Löffelbiskuit
100 g Sahne
500 g Magerquark, 20% Fett i. Tr.
70 g Zucker
2 TL (1 Pck.) Vanillezucker
1–2 EL Zitronensaft
3–4 EL gehackte Haselnüsse oder geröstete Mandelblättchen

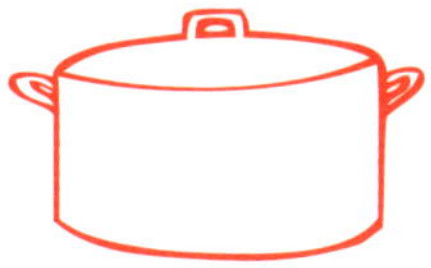

AUSSERDEM 1 kleine Auflaufform oder 1 flache Schüssel

ZUBEREITUNG

Die Äpfel mit wenig Wasser in einen Topf geben. Zimtstange und Zitronenviertel zugeben und das Ganze bei kleiner Hitze köcheln lassen, bis die Äpfel weich sind. Zimtstange und Zitrone entfernen und die Äpfel mit einem Kochlöffel zu einem groben Mus zerdrücken.
Den Apfelsaft in eine Schüssel füllen und die Löffelbiskuits einzeln durch den Saft ziehen. Den Boden einer kleinen Auflaufform mit den Löffelbiskuits auslegen. Sahne steif schlagen und beiseitestellen. Magerquark mit Zucker, Vanillezucker und Zitronensaft zu einer cremigen Masse verrühren. Die Hälfte der geschlagenen Sahne kräftig unterrühren, den Rest sachte unterziehen.
Einige Esslöffel der Creme dünn über die Biskuits streichen. Dann das Apfelmus darüber verteilen. Die restliche Quarkcreme über den Äpfeln verstreichen und das Tiramisu für ca. 1 Stunde abgedeckt in den Kühlschrank stellen. Zum Servieren mit gehackten Haselnüssen oder gerösteten Mandelblättchen bestreuen.

Tipp Wenn es mal schnell gehen soll, lässt sich das Apfeltiramisu auch mit gekauftem Apfelmus aus dem Glas rasch zaubern.

APPLE TIRAMISU

Preparation time approx. 30 minutes + 1 hour resting time

INGREDIENTS

1 1/2 lb apples, peeled, pitted and chopped into small pieces
1 cinnamon stick
1/4 of an untreated lemon
approx. 1/2 cup apple juice
7 oz ladyfingers
approx. 1/2 cup cream
2 cups low-fat curd cheese
1/4 cup sugar
2 tsp (1 sachet) vanilla sugar
1–2 Tb lemon juice
3–4 Tb ground hazelnuts or roasted almond flakes

IN ADDITION 1 small casserole dish or a shallow bowl

METHOD

Place the apples into a pot with a little water; add cinnamon stick and lemon and simmer over low heat until the apples are soft and begin to fall apart. After removing the cinnamon stick and lemon, use a wooden spoon to mash the apples into a coarse apple sauce. Pour the apple juice into a bowl and dredge the ladyfingers through the juice one by one. Line the bottom of the casserole with the ladyfingers. Whip the cream until stiff and set aside. Stir the curd cheese with the sugar, vanilla sugar and lemon juice until creamy. Mix in half of the whipped cream thoroughly; fold in the remaining half gently. Spread several tablespoons of the curd cheese mixture over the ladyfingers in a thin layer. Then daub the apple sauce over the cream. Spread the remaining curd cheese mixture evenly over the applesauce layer; refrigerate to set for about 1 hour. Garnish with the ground hazelnuts or roasted almond flakes.

Tips & Hints And when you are in a real hurry, the apple tiramisu can also be made with the store-bought apple sauce and is also still very enjoyable.

ARME RITTER

Ergibt 8 Stück
Zubereitungszeit ca. 30 Minuten

Die Bezeichnung »Arme Ritter« für dieses zugegebenermaßen recht schlichte Gericht tauchte erstmals im 14. Jahrhundert in einem deutschen Kochbuch auf. Manche Geschichtsforscher gehen davon aus, dass auf den Banketten des Mittelalters die höhergestellten Edelmänner mit Fleisch, Fisch und Pasteten verköstigt wurden, während die Knappen und das arme Fußvolk an den Nebentischen mit trockenem Brot, das in Milch getaucht und anschließend im heißen Fett ausgebacken wurde, vorliebnehmen mussten.
Auch Namen wie »Bavesen«, »Semmelschnitten« oder »Rostige Ritter« sind bis heute im Umlauf. Ersetzt man die Milch durch Rotwein, der zuvor mit Nelken und Zimt aromatisiert wurde, wird aus dem »Armen Ritter« übrigens eine »Versoffene Jungfrau«.

ZUTATEN

4 altbackene Semmeln oder 8 dicke Scheiben altbackenes Weißbrot

ZUM EINWEICHEN

3 Eigelb
2 EL Zucker
1 Prise Salz
Abrieb von 1/2 unbehandelten Zitrone
500 ml lauwarme Milch

FÜR DIE PANADE

3 Eiweiß
2 EL Wasser
200–250 g Semmelbrösel

AUSSERDEM 3 EL Butterschmalz, 100 g Zucker, 1 TL Zimtpulver, Küchentuch zum Abtropfen

ZUBEREITUNG

Die Semmeln entrinden und halbieren (die Weißbrotscheiben entrinden). Eigelbe mit Zucker, Salz, Zitronenabrieb und Milch in eine Schüssel geben und miteinander verquirlen.
In einer zweiten Schüssel die Eiweiße mit Wasser verrühren. Die Semmelbrösel in eine dritte Schüssel geben.
Nun die Semmelscheiben in der Eiermilch 1–2 Minuten lang einweichen, dabei öfters wenden. Dann die Semmeln im

GRILLED CINNAMON TOAST

Yields 8 pieces of toast
Preparation time approx. 30 minutes

The term for this rather simple dish – "Arme Ritter," which literally means "poor knights," surfaced for the first time in the 14th century in a German cookbook. Some historians assume that the nobility of the Middle Ages were served meat, fish, and meat pies at the banquets while the squires and poor peasants had to make due with dry bread that had been dipped in milk and then fried in hot fat. Names such as "Bavesen," "Semmelschnitten" (literally: bread slices) or "Rostiger Ritter" (literally: rusty knight) are still used today. By the way, if you replace the ingredient milk with red wine, which was previously flavored with cloves and cinnamon, the "poor knight" turns into a "Versoffene Jungfrau" (literally: drunken virgin).

INGREDIENTS

4 stale rolls or 8 thick slices of white bread

FOR SOAKING

3 egg yolks
2 Tb sugar
1 pinch salt
grated rind of 1/2 lemon
2 cups lukewarm milk

FOR DREDGING

3 egg whites
2 Tb water
approx. 1 cup dried breadcrumbs

IN ADDITION 5 Tb clarified butter, 1/3 cup sugar, 1 tsp ground cinnamon, paper towel for draining

METHOD

Grate off the crust of the rolls (if you chose to use white bread: also remove the crust); then halve like a sandwich. Place the egg yolks, sugar, salt, lemon rind and milk into a bowl and mix.
In another bowl, mix the egg whites with the water. Put the breadcrumbs in a third bowl.
Soak the roll halves in the egg and milk mixture for 1–2 minutes repeatedly turning them over. Dip the rolls into the egg

Eiweißgemisch wenden und zum Schluss in den Semmelbröseln panieren.
Das Butterschmalz in einer Pfanne erhitzen und die Armen Ritter darin goldbraun backen. Auf dem bereitgelegten Küchentuch abtropfen lassen. Wenn nötig, während des Backens noch mal Butterschmalz zugeben.
Zucker und Zimt miteinander verrühren. Zum Servieren die Armen Ritter auf vorgewärmten Tellern verteilen; großzügig mit dem Zimt-Zucker-Gemisch bestreuen. Heiß servieren!

Tipp Zu Armen Rittern passt am besten Apfelmus. Für Eilige auch gerne aus dem Glas.

whites and then dredge them in the breadcrumbs. Melt the clarified butter in a pan and fry the roll halves until golden brown. If necessary, add more clarified butter. Drain on a paper towel. Mix the sugar and cinnamon together. Place the roll halves onto a warm plate and generously sprinkle with the cinnamon sugar. Serve hot.

Tips & Hints Grilled cinnamon toast is best enjoyed with apple sauce. Apple sauce can also just be bought in a jar for those of you who are pressed for time or simply used to convenience of prepared food.

BAYERISCH CREME

Zubereitungszeit insgesamt ca. 45 Minuten +
3 Stunden Kühlzeit

Die Bayerisch Creme ist der Klassiker schlechthin unter den bayerischen Desserts. Aber sagen Sie das bloß keinem Engländer, auf der Insel ist diese Sünde nämlich unter dem Namen »Englische Creme« bekannt.
Allerdings spricht doch sehr viel für die bayerische Namensgebung, denn bereits im 14. Jahrhundert ließ sich der Herzog von Bayern-Ingolstadt diese an sich eher schlichte Eiercreme ziemlich oft zum Nachtisch kredenzen. Als sich seine Tochter schließlich 1385 mit dem französischen König vermählte, erfuhr die Bayerisch Creme einen fulminanten Aufstieg in die Haute Cuisine, denn die schöne Isabeau wollte ohne diese sinnliche Süßigkeit ihre Heimat partout nicht verlassen und brachte das Rezept mit an den königlichen Hof ihres Gemahls.

ZUTATEN

4 Blatt Gelatine
500 ml Milch
1 Vanilleschote
6 Eigelb
90 g Zucker
600 g Sahne

ZUBEREITUNG

Die Gelatine in einer Schüssel mit kaltem Wasser einweichen lassen und beiseitestellen. Milch in einen Topf geben. Die Vanilleschote mit einem scharfen Messer einritzen, zur Milch geben und zusammen zum Kochen bringen.
Währenddessen Eigelb und Zucker in einer Schüssel schaumig rühren.
Die heiße Milch durch ein Sieb über die Ei-Zucker-Masse gießen.
Anschließend in einem kleinen Topf zwei bis drei Fingerbreit Wasser zum Kochen bringen. Die Eiermasse in der Schüssel über dem Wasserdampf 15 Minuten lang mit einem Schneebesen beständig rühren. Dabei darauf achten, dass der Boden der Schüssel nicht mit dem Wasser in Berührung kommt.
Hat sich die Masse verdickt und bilden sich beim Schlagen mit dem Schneebesen zarte Muster, ist sie fertig und kann beiseitegestellt werden. Ca. 15–20 Minuten abkühlen lassen.

BAVARIAN CREAM

Total preparation time approx. 45 minutes +
3 hours to set and chill

The Bavarian cream is the classic par excellence among Bavarian desserts. But don't ever say that in earshot of an English person; on their island, this sinful sweet is known as "Crème Anglaise" (French for "English cream").
However, there is a strong case for the Bavarian naming because in the 14th century the Duke of Bavaria-Ingolstadt had already had this inherently rather simple egg custard served for dessert quite often. When his daughter finally married the French king in 1385, the Bavarian cream ascended to a Grande Cuisine because the beautiful Isabeau refused to leave her homeland without this tempting dessert and brought the recipe along with her to her husband's royal court.

INGREDIENTS

1 package of gelatin
2 1/4 cups milk
1 vanilla bean
6 egg yolks
1/4 cup plus 1 Tb sugar
2 1/2 cups cream

METHOD

Soften the gelatin in cold water and set aside. Pour milk into a pot; score the vanilla bean with a knife, then add to milk and bring to a boil.
Meanwhile, whip the egg yolks and sugar in a bowl until frothy. Strain the hot milk into the bowl with the eggs and sugar. Bring one to two finger's width of water to a boil in a small pot. Set the bowl with the custard over the top of the pot and whisk the mixture constantly for about 15 minutes. Make sure the bottom of the bowl never touches the water. When the custard has thickened and the whisk leaves behind a soft trail, it is done and can be set aside. Let cool for about 15–20 minutes.
Whip the cream until stiff. Remove gelatin from water, strain properly and mix with the custard. Then gently fold the whipped cream into the custard.
Put little portions of the Bavarian cream into dessert dishes or parfait glasses and refrigerate for about 3 hours until set.

Anschließend die Sahne steif schlagen. Dann die Gelatine aus dem Wasser nehmen, gut ausdrücken und unter die Creme rühren. Zum Schluss die Sahne unterheben.
Die Bayerisch Creme portionsweise in Gläser oder Schälchen füllen und für ca. 3 Stunden in den Kühlschrank stellen.

Tipps

* *Keine Angst vor Gelatine, sie ist ganz leicht zu handhaben! Grundsätzlich gilt: Weichen Sie die Blätter in so kaltem Wasser wie möglich ein und halten Sie sich an die Einweichzeit auf der Packung. Gut ausdrücken und wie im Rezept oben angegeben weiterverarbeiten.*
* *In manchen Restaurants und heimischen Küchen wird die Bayerisch Creme heutzutage auch mit Agar-Agar zubereitet, einer Art pflanzlichem Geliermittel aus getrockneten Meeralgen. Ich selbst habe noch keine nennenswerten Erfahrungen damit gemacht – probieren Sie's aus!*
* *Eine klassische Bayerisch Creme wird traditionell mit frischen Beeren der Saison wie z. B. Erd-, Blau- oder Himbeeren serviert. Aber auch lauwarmes Rhabarber- oder Zwetschgenkompott schmeckt himmlisch dazu.*

Tips & Hints

* *No need to fear gelatin; it is very easy to use. A rule of thumb: Soak the leaves in water that is as cold as possible and adhere to the instructions on its soaking time on the package. Strain well and proceed further as described in the recipe above.*
* *Nowadays, agar agar, which is a kind of vegetable gelling agent made from dried marine algae, is also used to replace the gelatin when making Bavarian cream in some restaurants and home kitchens. I myself haven't tried this yet – give it a shot.*
* *A classic Bavarian cream is traditionally served with fresh seasonal berries, such as strawberries, blueberries or raspberries. Lukewarm rhubarb or plum compote also go very well with it.*

DAMPFNUDELN MIT VANILLESOSSE

Zubereitungszeit inkl. Ruhezeit für den Hefeteig ca. 1,5 Stunden

Dampfnudeln kamen früher, gerade in den ländlichen Regionen Bayerns, recht häufig auf den Tisch. Man aß sie in der Regel als deftige Variante zum Mittagessen mit Sauerkraut oder geschmortem Kohlrabi – beides wurde gemeinsam mit den Dampfnudeln in einem Topf gegart – oder in heißes Butterschmalz getaucht. Süße Dampfnudeln kamen hingegen sonntags zum Nachmittagskaffee auf den Tisch, dann in Begleitung von gekochtem und leicht gesüßtem Obst oder mit einer Art Milchsuppe, der Vorreiterin unserer nachstehenden Vanillesoße.

ZUTATEN

FÜR DEN VORTEIG
ca. 30 g frische Hefe
3 EL lauwarme Milch
1 Prise Zucker
1 gehäufter EL Mehl

FÜR DEN TEIG
500 g Mehl
1 Ei
ca. 250 ml lauwarme Milch
ca. 50 g zerlassene Butter
1/2 TL Abrieb einer unbehandelten Zitrone

FÜR DIE VANILLESOSSE
1 l Vollmilch
2 Vanilleschoten
4 Eigelb
40 g Stärke
100 g Zucker
1/8 l Vollmilch
1 EL Zucker
1 EL Butter

ZUM KOCHEN DER DAMPFNUDELN
Milch
80 g Zucker
1 EL Butter

AUSSERDEM Mehl zum Bestäuben der Arbeitsfläche, 1 großer, dicht schließender Topf

STEAMED YEAST CAKES WITH VANILLA CUSTARD

Preparation time including resting time approx. 1.5 hours

"Dampfnudeln" were often served in the old days, especially in peasant regions of Bavaria. It was common to either eat them as a solid lunch with sauerkraut or stewed kohlrabi, which were both cooked in a pot with the yeast cakes, or merely dunked in melted clarified butter. The sweet version was usually served with Sunday's afternoon coffee with slightly sweetened fruit or a kind of milk soup – the forerunner of today's usual vanilla custard, which is described below.

INGREDIENTS

FOR THE YEAST STARTER
1/4 cup yeast
3 Tb lukewarm milk
1 pinch sugar
1 Tb flour

FOR THE DOUGH
4 cups flour
1 egg
approx. 2 cups lukewarm milk
approx. 3 1/3 Tb melted butter
1/2 tsp grated lemon rind

FOR THE VANILLA CUSTARD
5 cups whole milk
2 vanilla beans
4 egg yolks
2 1/2 Tb starch
1/2 cup sugar
1/2 cup whole milk
1 Tb sugar
2 Tb butter

FOR THE COOKING OF THE YEAST CAKES
milk
1/4 cup sugar
2 Tb butter

IN ADDITION flour for dusting the work surface, 1 large sealable, lidded pot

ZUBEREITUNG

Die Hefe mit den Fingern zerbröseln und in eine große Schüssel geben. Die restlichen Zutaten für den Vorteig zugeben und gut verrühren. Die Schüssel mit einem Geschirrtuch abdecken und an einen warmen Ort stellen. Den Vorteig ca. 15 Minuten gehen lassen, damit sich das sogenannte »Dampferl« bilden kann.

Dann die Zutaten für den Teig nach und nach zum Vorteig geben und alles zu einem geschmeidigen Teig verkneten; dabei den Teig immer wieder fest auf die Arbeitsfläche schlagen, damit sich kleine Luftkammern bilden können. Den Teig wieder in die Schüssel geben und erneut zugedeckt 30–40 Minuten an einem warmen, nicht zugigen Ort gehen lassen.

Anschließend den Teig in kleine Bälle portionieren – etwa so groß wie ein Hühnerei – und dann auf eine bemehlte Arbeitsfläche legen. Erneut mit einem Küchentuch abdecken und noch mal 20 Minuten gehen lassen.

Danach Milch etwa 3 cm hoch in den Topf füllen; Zucker und Butter unterrühren und alles zusammen auf kleiner Flamme erhitzen. Teigstücke nebeneinander in die Flüssigkeit setzen und weiterhin auf kleiner Flamme und gut verschlossen (es darf kein Dampf entweichen) ca. 10–12 Minuten garen.

Währenddessen 1 l Milch für die Vanillesoße mit den Vanilleschoten (Schoten vorher mit einem scharfen Messer einritzen) aufkochen lassen. Bis die Milch kocht, Eigelbe, Stärke, 100 g Zucker und 1/8 l Milch in einer Schüssel miteinander verrühren und dann in die heiße Vanillemilch geben. Einige Minuten sanft köcheln lassen und zum Schluss je 1 Esslöffel Zucker und Butter mit einem Schneebesen unterrühren.

Tipps

* *Statt in einem gezuckerten Milchbad können Sie Ihre Dampfnudeln auch in starkem Kaffee garen. Dazu Espresso oder sehr starken Kaffee aufbrühen, großzügig zuckern und noch heiß in den Topf geben (ca. 3 cm hoch). Teigbälle einsetzen und weiter wie oben verfahren.*
* *Werfen Sie die Vanilleschoten nach dem Aufkochen nicht weg, denn mit ihnen lässt sich ganz leicht Vanillezucker herstellen. Dazu die Vanilleschoten unter klarem Wasser abspülen, auskratzen und anschließend trocknen lassen. Die Schoten zusammen mit Zucker in ein gut verschließbares Glas geben. Wird Ihnen nach einiger Zeit der Duft zu intensiv, einfach die Schoten entfernen. Faustregel: Je mehr Vanilleschoten, desto intensiver schmeckt und duftet der Vanillezucker.*

METHOD

Crumble yeast into a bowl. Add the remaining ingredients for the yeast starter and mix well. Cover the bowl with a kitchen towel; place in a warm spot for about 15 minutes until the "Dampferl" – as the starter is called in Bavaria – begins to produce tiny bubbles.

Gradually add the ingredients for the dough to the yeast starter; knead it into a smooth dough, repeatedly slamming it onto your work surface. This causes the dough to develop tiny air pockets, lending it a nice thick consistency. Cover and let rise 30–40 minutes. After the dough has risen, cut out egg-sized pieces and place them on a floured work surface. Cover with a towel and let the dough rise for another 20 minutes.

Place about an inch of milk, sugar and butter into a heavy pot and set over low heat. Place the pieces of dough next to one another in the milk and cover. (Do not allow any steam to escape.) Steam over low heat for about 10–12 minutes.

Meanwhile prepare the vanilla sauce. Bring 4 cups milk to a simmer with the vanilla beans. While the milk is warming, mix the egg yolks, starch, sugar and 1/2 cup milk in a bowl; then add the contents to the hot milk. Let simmer for a few minutes and finish by stirring in the butter.

Tips & Hints

* *Alternatively to cooking the "Dampfnudeln" in sugary milk, you can try cooking them in strong coffee. Brew espresso or very strong coffee and generously add sugar and pour into a pot (approx. 1 1/5 inches high) while still hot. Place the pieces of dough next to one another in the coffee and proceed further as is described above.*
* *Do not discard the vanilla beans after boiling because vanilla sugar can be made at home quite easily with them. Rinse the vanilla beans under clear water, scrape them out and then let them dry. Add the dried vanilla beans to sugar in a sealable jar or container. If the smell becomes too intense after some time, just remove the beans. Rule of thumb: The more vanilla beans are added, the more intense the taste and smell of the vanilla sugar will become.*

G'STECKELTE MILCH MIT FRÜCHTEN DER SAISON

Zubereitungszeit 5–10 Minuten + ein paar Tage, die die frische Milch braucht, um zu stocken

Für dieses uralte Rezept brauchen Sie in erster Linie einen Bauern Ihres Vertrauens, der frische, nicht pasteurisierte Kuhmilch direkt ab Hof verkauft. Städter haben es da zugegebenermaßen etwas schwer, aber der Aufwand, extra dafür aufs Land hinauszufahren, lohnt sich allemal! Verbinden Sie das Ganze doch mit einem schönen Familienausflug und zeigen Sie Ihren Kindern, wo die Milch wirklich herkommt.

ZUTATEN

1 l absolut frische, nicht pasteurisierte Vollmilch
1 kg Früchte der Saison, z. B. Erdbeeren, Aprikosen, Zwetschgen, Kirschen usw., gewaschen und zum Verzehr verarbeitet
ca. 2–3 EL Zucker

ZUBEREITUNG

Die Milch in eine Porzellan- oder Steingutschüssel geben und an einen kühlen Ort ohne direkte Sonneneinstrahlung stellen. Nicht zudecken! Nach einigen Tagen – manchmal schon nach einem Tag – stockt sie. Nun die g'steckelte Milch für 1 Stunde in den Kühlschrank stellen.
Früchte zum Verzehr vorbereiten und in eine große Schale oder Schüssel geben, mit Zucker bestreuen. Die g'steckelte Milch darübergeben und gleich servieren. Ein wunderbar erfrischendes Sommerdessert!

Tipp G'steckelte Milch schmeckt auch pur, nur mit einem Hauch von Zimt und Zucker bestreut, sehr lecker.

CLABBERED MILK WITH SEASONAL FRUIT

Preparation time 5–10 minutes + a couple of days that the fresh milk needs to increase

For this ancient recipe, you will need a farmer you trust, who sells unpasteurized cow milk direct from the farm, fresh first and foremost. It is admittedly somewhat more difficult from the city, but always worth the effort, to drive especially out to the country. Combine it with a nice family trip and show your children where milk really comes from.

INGREDIENTS

5 cups absolutely fresh, unpasteurized milk
6 1/2 cups fruits of the season, such as strawberries, apricots, plums, cherries, etc., washed and processed for human consumption
about 2–3 Tb sugar

METHOD

Contain the milk in a porcelain or earthen ware bowl and set in a cool place away from direct sunlight. Do not cover. After a few days – sometimes after a day – it will be ready to use. Now leave the clabbered milk in the fridge for 1 hour.
Prepare fruits for consumption and serve in a large dish or bowl; sprinkle with sugar. Add the clabbered milk and serve immediately. A wonderfully refreshing summer dessert.

Tips & Hints Although clabbered milk tastes so good pure, adding a hint of cinnamon and sugar can create a new taste experience.

HOLLERKÜCHERL

Zubereitungszeit inkl. Ruhezeit für den Teig ca. 35 Minuten

Hollerküchерl haben im Jahreslauf nur kurz Saison, dann nämlich, wenn sich an den Zweigen des Holunderstrauchs hübsche, weiße Blütendolden gebildet haben. Der Holunder blüht etwa von Ende Mai bis Ende Juni; seine zart duftenden Blüten schmecken leicht herb und gelten unter Kennern als Delikatesse. Übrigens, ein alter bayerischer Brauch besagt, dass es Glück bringt, wenn man vor einem Holunderstrauch drei Mal hintereinander den Hut zieht!

ZUTATEN

FÜR DEN TEIG

ca. 180 g Mehl
1/4 l Milch
2 Eier
1 Prise Salz
8 große Holunderblütendolden, gewaschen und gut abgetropft

AUSSERDEM Butter zum Ausbacken, Puderzucker zum Bestäuben

ZUBEREITUNG

Alle Zutaten für den Teig in einer Schüssel miteinander verrühren, sodass eine Art zäher Pfannkuchenteig entsteht. Ca. 15–20 Minuten ruhen lassen.

Butter in einer Pfanne erhitzen (ca. 1 EL auf zwei Blütendolden). Die Dolden portionsweise durch den Teig ziehen, dabei darauf achten, dass recht viel Teig an den Blüten hängen bleibt. Die Dolden mit dem Stiel nach oben in der Pfanne backen, bis der Teig eine goldgelbe Farbe angenommen hat. So verfahren, bis alle Dolden gebacken sind. Noch warm mit Puderzucker bestäuben und gleich servieren.

Tipps

* *Sie können Ihre Hollerküchерl auch in einem Bierteig backen. Auf diese Form der Zubereitung schwören viele bayerische Süßmäuler! Dazu einfach die Milch im Rezept für den Teig durch Bier ersetzen und dann genauso weitermachen, wie im Rezept oben angegeben. Das Bier verleiht den herben Hollerblüten eine wunderbar malzige Note.*

FRIED ELDERFLOWER PASTRY

Preparation time including resting time for the dough approx. 35 minutes

Elderberries have only a short season in the course of the year, and start as beautiful white flower clusters (umbels) on the branches of the elderberry bush. The elderberry flowers bloom from approximately the end of May until the end of June; these delicately scented flowers with a slightly bitter taste are considered a delicacy among connoisseurs. By the way, an old Bavarian custom says that it brings good luck if one takes off their hat in front of an elderberry bush three times in a row.

INGREDIENTS

FOR THE DOUGH

approx. 1 1/2 cups flour
1 cup milk
2 eggs
1 pinch salt
8 great elderflower umbels, washed and well drained

IN ADDITION butter for frying, powdered sugar for dusting

METHOD

Mix all the ingredients for the dough in a bowl together, creating a kind of tough, stiff batter. Leave rest for 15–20 minutes.

Heat butter in a frying pan (about 1 Tb on two flower umbels). Draw the umbels through the batter, making sure that it sticks pretty well on the flowers. Bake these batter-covered umbels with stem facing upwards in the baking pan, until the dough has reached a golden yellow color. Do this until all cones are baked. Still warm, dust with powdered sugar and serve immediately.

Tips & Hints

* *You can also bake elderberries in a beer batter. Many Bavarians with a sweet tooth swear by this form of preparation. Simply replace the milk in the recipe for the dough with beer and then just continue as indicated in the recipe above. The beer adds a wonderfully malted taste to the elderberry flowers.*

SCHOKOMILLISEMMERL MIT LAUWARMEM APFELTAUCH

Ergibt 8 Stück
Zubereitungszeit insgesamt 20 Minuten + 25 Minuten Backzeit + 12 Stunden Kühlzeit für den Teig

Das Rezept für die Millisemmerl stammt von zwei hochbetagten Schwestern, Zwillingen, die gemeinsam einen Bauernhof im oberbayerischen Voralpenland bewirtschaften. Ich verbrachte einmal ein ganzes Wochenende bei ihnen, um mich in die Geheimnisse bäuerlicher Mehlspeisen einführen zu lassen. Im nachstehenden Rezept habe ich den Semmerl noch eine Füllung aus Schokolade verpasst, aber auch pur schmecken sie wunderbar. Die Idee, das Ganze wie ein süß belegtes Brötchen zu servieren, kam uns dreien zu vorgerückter Stunde nach etlichen Stamperln Schnaps in der gemütlichen Kuchl des alten Einödhofs – wir finden es köstlich so!

ZUTATEN

FÜR DEN TEIG
100 g Butter, zimmerwarm
500 g Mehl
4 TL Backpulver
2 TL Zucker
1 Prise Salz
300 ml lauwarme Milch
100 g Zartbitterschokolade, fein zerbröselt
1 Eigelb zum Bestreichen der Semmerl

FÜR DEN TAUCH
1 TL Puderzucker
1 EL Butter
4 mittelgroße säuerliche Äpfel, gewaschen, vom Kerngehäuse befreit und in schmale Spalten geschnitten
ca. 3 EL Aprikosenmarmelade
1 Zimtstange

AUSSERDEM Frischhaltefolie, 200 g Sahne

ZUBEREITUNG
Alle Zutaten für den Teig – außer der Schokolade und dem Eigelb – in einer Schüssel miteinander vermengen und zu einem festen, geschmeidigen Teig kneten. Anschließend die

CHOCOLATE MILK ROLLS WITH APPLE DIP

Yields 8 pieces
Total preparation time 20 minutes + 25 minutes baking time + 12 hours cooling time for the dough

The recipe for the milk rolls comes from two elderly sisters, twins, who manage a farm together in the foothills of Bavaria. I spent an entire weekend with them so they would introduce to me the secrets of peasant pastries. In the following recipe, I have filled the roll with chocolate, but they also taste wonderful in their pure form. We had the idea of serving the whole thing like a sweet sandwich late in the evening after having enjoyed several brandys together in the cozy corner in the old "Einödhof," that secluded farm – we find it delicious.

INGREDIENTS

FOR THE DOUGH
7 Tb butter at room temperature
4 cups flour
4 tsp baking powder
2 tsp sugar
1 pinch salt
1 cup lukewarm milk
1 cup dark chocolate, finely crushed and ground
1 egg yolk for brushing the bread

FOR THE DIP
1 tsp powdered sugar
2 Tb butter
4 medium tart apples, washed, freed from the cores and cut into wedges
about 3 Tb apricot jam
1 cinnamon stick

IN ADDITION clear platic wrap, scant 1 cup cream

METHOD
Knead all the ingredients for the dough – except the chocolate and the egg yolk –, in a bowl and form a smooth dough. Then wrap the ball of dough firmly in plastic wrap and place in the refrigerator for 12 hours, for best results leave it overnight. The next day, preheat the oven to 350°F. Knead the dough again, work in the chocolate chips, and then roll to a thick strand. Split the roll of dough into 8 equal pieces (each approx.

Teigkugel fest in Frischhaltefolie packen und für 12 Stunden, am besten über Nacht, in den Kühlschrank legen.
Am nächsten Tag den Backofen auf 180 Grad vorheizen. Den Teig noch mal gut durchkneten, dabei die Schokoladenstückchen mit einarbeiten, und dann zu einem dicken Strang rollen. Die Teigrolle in 8 gleich große Stücke teilen (pro Stück ca. 125 g) und die Teigstücke dann zu kleinen Bällchen formen. Die Bälle auf ein mit Backpapier ausgelegtes Backblech legen und die Oberflächen mit Eigelb bestreichen. Die Millisemmerl ca. 25 Minuten goldgelb backen. Die Semmeln sind fertig, wenn sie beim Klopfen mit dem Fingerknöchel auf der Unterseite hohl klingen.
Während die Semmerl leicht auskühlen, eine große Pfanne trocken auf dem Herd erhitzen. Darin den Puderzucker karamellisieren bzw. schmelzen lassen. Dabei darauf achten, dass der Zucker nicht schwarz, sondern nur leicht braun wird, sonst wird der »Tauch« bitter und ungenießbar. Butter zugeben und zergehen lassen. Die Apfelspalten unter mehrmaligem Rühren darin dünsten, bis sie weich sind. Aprikosenmarmelade unterrühren und Zimtstange zugeben. Ca. 2 Minuten köcheln lassen, bis sich die Marmelade verflüssigt hat.
Zum Servieren die noch lauwarmen Millisemmerl in der Mitte durchschneiden, auf die Unterseite flüssige Sahne gießen und mit Apfeltauch belegen. Dann mit der Semmeloberseite, wie bei einem belegten Brötchen, abdecken.

Tipps

- *Millisemmerl lassen sich auch wunderbar mit gefrorenen Himbeeren füllen. Die Himbeeren dazu vor dem Backen ganz sanft in die fertigen Teigbälle drücken.*
- *Auch Rosinen, die zuvor über Nacht in Hochprozentigem oder schlicht in Orangensaft eingeweicht werden, eignen sich sehr gut, um die Semmerl noch etwas aufzupeppen.*

125 g) and with the dough pieces then form small balls. Place the balls on a baking sheet lined with parchment paper and sprinkle the surface with egg yolk. Bake the milk rolls until golden for about 25 minutes. The cakes are done when they sound hollow after tapping the bottom of them with your knuckles.
While the bread cools slightly, heat a large, dry pan on the stove. Then caramelize and melt the sugar. Be sure that the sugar is lightly brown but not black, otherwise it will become bitter and inedible. Add and melt butter. Sauté the apple slices in it while repeatedly stirring until they are soft. Stir apricot jam and add the cinnamon stick. Simmer for 2 minutes, until the jam has liquefied.
To serve, cut through the middle of the still lukewarm milk rolls, pour cream on the bottom of the roll and spread apple dip on it. Then cover with the top of the roll, like when filling bread rolls.

Tips & Hints

- *Milk rolls can also be filled with frozen raspberries. Gently press the raspberries before baking in the finished dough balls.*
- *Also raisins, which are soaked overnight in brandy or simply orange juice, are very good to spice up the rolls.*

ZWETSCHGENKNÖDEL

Zubereitungszeit ca. 45–60 Minuten

ZUTATEN

FÜR DEN TEIG

200 g Grieß
200 g Mehl
500 g Quark, 40% Fett i. Tr.
2 Eier
1 Prise Salz

FÜR DIE FÜLLUNG

ca. 750 g Zwetschgen, gewaschen und entsteint; dabei darauf achten, dass die Früchte an einer »Naht« zusammenbleiben, sodass Sie sie wieder zuklappen können
Würfelzucker
1 Prise Salz
ca. 80 g Butter
ca. 100 g Semmelbrösel
Zimt-Zucker-Gemisch

AUSSERDEM 1 große Pfanne, 1 großer Topf, Salz

ZUBEREITUNG

Alle Zutaten für den Teig in eine Schüssel geben und gut miteinander vermengen.
Jeweils eine Zwetschge mit Würfelzucker füllen und die Frucht wieder zusammenklappen.
Reichlich Wasser auf dem Herd zum Kochen bringen und salzen. Dann die Hitze reduzieren, sodass das Wasser nur noch leicht simmert.
Den Teig um die einzelnen Zwetschgen herum zu klebrigen Knödeln formen und die Knödel im simmernden Wasser ca. 10–15 Minuten gar ziehen lassen.
Daneben Butter in der Pfanne erhitzen und die Semmelbrösel goldbraun anrösten. Die fertigen Zwetschgenknödel zum Servieren in tiefe Teller geben und mit den heißen Semmelbröseln aus der Pfanne bedecken. Zum Abschluss Zimt und Zucker darüberstreuen.

Tipp Die Knödel lassen sich auch wunderbar mit Aprikosen oder Mirabellen füllen.

PLUM DUMPLINGS

Preparation time approx. 45–60 minutes

INGREDIENTS

FOR THE DOUGH

1 cup semolina
1 3/5 cups flour
2 cups curd cheese
2 eggs
1 pinch salt

FOR THE FILLING

approx. 5 1/4 cups plums, washed and pitted. Be sure that the fruits remain attached at their "seam," so that you can open them again
cube sugar
1 pinch salt
approx. 5 1/2 Tb butter
approx. 6 Tb breadcrumbs
cinnamon-sugar mixture

IN ADDITION 1 large pan, 1 large pot, salt

METHOD

Mix all the ingredients for the dough in a bowl.
Fill each plum with sugar cubes and fold the fruit again.
Boil plenty of water with salt on the stove. Then reduce the heat so that the water is only slightly simmering.
Wrap the dough around the individual plums to sticky dumplings and soak the dumplings in simmering water for about 10–15 minutes. Melt butter in the frying pan and toast breadcrumbs until golden brown. Serve plum dumplings in deep dishes and cover with the hot breadcrumbs out of the pan. To complete the dish sprinkle with cinnamon and sugar.

Tips & Hints The dumplings are also wonderful with an apricot or mirabelle filling.

TOPFENNOCKERL NR. 1

Zubereitungszeit ca. 30 Minuten

Traditionelle Topfennockerl sind für sich gesehen eine etwas neutrale Angelegenheit, deswegen habe ich dieses alte Rezept, das von einer Bäuerin aus dem bayerischen Voralpenland stammt, mit etwas Orangenmehl aufgepeppt. Ohne süße Begleitung wie Früchtekompott oder einem schlichten Zimt-Zucker-Gemisch kommen die Nockerl aber trotzdem nicht aus!

ZUTATEN

250 g trockener Topfen (Magerquark), 20% Fett i. Tr. – gegebenenfalls noch mal durch ein Küchentuch ausdrücken
2 Eier
4 EL Mehl
1 Prise Salz
1 Msp. Orangenmehl (s. Husarenknöpferl S. 129)

AUSSERDEM ca. 50 g Butter, Zucker und Zimt zum Bestreuen der Nockerl

ZUBEREITUNG

Den Topfen in eine Schüssel geben und mit den Eiern, dem Mehl, der Prise Salz und dem Orangenmehl gut verrühren. Reichlich Wasser in einem großen Topf erhitzen und anschließend mit zwei Teelöffeln, die zwischendurch immer wieder in kaltes Wasser getaucht werden, Nockerl formen. Die Nockerl im siedenden Wasser ca. 10 Minuten gar ziehen lassen und dann gut abtropfen lassen.
Anschließend Butter in einer Pfanne erhitzen und die Topfennockerl in der heißen Butter schwenken. Mit Zimt und Zucker bestreuen und noch warm servieren.

Tipp Zu den Topfennockerl passt auch wunderbar der lauwarme Apfeltauch aus dem Rezept für die Schokomillisemmerl (s. S. 106). Oder Sie kombinieren Ihre Nockerl mit dem Rhabarberkompott aus dem Rezept für den Grießschmarrn (s. S. 30).

CURD CHEESE DUMPLINGS NO. 1

Preparation time approx. 30 minutes

Traditional curd cheese dumplings are a somewhat neutral matter in itself, that's why I have jazzed up this old recipe that comes from a farmer's wife from the Bavarian Alps, with some orange flour. Without sweet compliments such as fruit compote or a simple mixture of cinnamon and sugar, the dumplings don't taste as good.

INGREDIENTS

1 cup dry low-fat curd cheese – if necessary, again pressed through a kitchen towel
2 eggs
4 Tb flour
1 pinch salt
1 pinch orange flour (cf. "Husarenknöpferl" pg. 129)

IN ADDITION approx. 3 Tb butter, sugar and cinnamon for sprinkling the dumplings

METHOD

Serve the curd cheese in a bowl and mix well with the eggs, the flour, the pinch of salt and the orange flour. Heat plenty of water in a large pot and leave two teaspoons immersed in cold water which are used to form the dumplings.
Leave the dumplings in boiling water for 10 minutes to soak and then drain.
Then heat butter in a pan and swirl the curd cheese dumplings in the hot butter. Sprinkle with cinnamon and sugar and serve while still warm.

Tips & Hints For the curd cheese dumplings, the lukewarm apple dip from the recipe for the "Schokomillisemmerl" (see pg. 106) is also well-suited or combine your dumplings with the rhubarb compote in the recipe for the semolina pancakes (see pg. 30)

TOPFENNOCKERL NR. 2

Zubereitungszeit inkl. Backzeit ca. 45 Minuten

ZUTATEN

FÜR DIE NOCKERL

500 g Topfen (Quark), 40% Fett i. Tr.
75 g Hartweizengrieß
75 g Mehl
3 Eier
Abrieb von 1 unbehandelten Zitrone
1 Prise Salz

FÜR DIE ZUCKERMILCH

1/4 l Vollmilch
60 g Zucker
2 TL (1 Pck.) Vanillezucker
60 g Butter, zimmerwarm

AUSSERDEM 1 Auflaufform, Butter zum Einfetten der Form

ZUBEREITUNG

Alle Zutaten für die Nockerl in einer Schüssel zu einem Teig verrühren. Die Zutaten für die Zuckermilch in einem Topf erhitzen und dann in die vorbereitete Auflaufform gießen.
Backofen auf 180 Grad vorheizen.
Mit zwei Esslöffeln Nockerl aus dem Teig abstechen und in die Zuckermilch setzen. In ca. 40 Minuten goldbraun backen.

Tipp Dazu passen eingelegte Früchte oder Früchtekompott.

CURD CHEESE DUMPLINGS NO. 2

Preparation time including baking time 45 minutes

INGREDIENTS

FOR THE DUMPLINGS

2 cups curd cheese
7 Tb durum wheat semolina
3/5 cup flour
3 eggs
grated rind of 1 untreated lemon
1 pinch salt

FOR THE SUGAR MILK

1 cup whole milk
5 Tb sugar
2 tsp (1 sachet) vanilla sugar
4 Tb butter at room temperature

IN ADDITION 1 baking dish, butter for greasing the form

METHOD

Stir all of the ingredients for the dumplings in a bowl to make a dough. Heat the ingredients for sugar milk in a pot and then pour into the prepared baking dish.
Preheat the oven to 350°F.
Using two tablespoons, cut off the dough and add it into the sugar milk. Bake for about 40 minutes until golden brown.

Tips & Hints To complement the dumplings use canned fruit or fruit compote.

ZITRONENCREME

Zubereitungszeit ca. 10 Minuten + 1 Stunde Kühlzeit

Als ich noch ein kleines Mädchen war, gab es für mich nichts Köstlicheres als die Zitronencreme meiner Großmutter. Leider ist Omi vor vielen Jahren gestorben und ich habe es versäumt, sie zu Lebzeiten nach dem Rezept zu fragen. Es hat einige Anläufe gebraucht, um die Creme originalgetreu hinzubekommen, aber ich bin mit dem Ergebnis zufrieden – und meine Oma im Himmel droben sicher auch. Das folgende Rezept ist für ca. acht Personen oder für vier mit Nachschlaggarantie!

ZUTATEN

250 g Mascarpone
500 g Magerquark, 20 % Fett i. Tr.
200 g Sahne
5 Pck. Vanillezucker
2 EL Zucker
ca. 100 ml Milch
Saft von ca. 3 Zitronen, je nach Geschmack
Abrieb von 1 unbehandelten Zitrone

ZUM GARNIEREN 1 Limette oder wahlweise 1 Zitrone, in Scheiben geschnitten, Honig, 1 EL gehackte Walnusskerne

ZUBEREITUNG

Alle Zutaten für die Creme nacheinander in eine große Schüssel geben (sehr hübsch macht sich die Zitronencreme in einer Glasschüssel) und zu einer glatten Masse verrühren. Zum Schluss Zitronensaft und Zitronenschalenabrieb unterrühren. Evtl. mit Zucker noch mal abschmecken.
Die Creme für ca. 60 Minuten kühl stellen. Zum Servieren mit Limettenscheiben, Honig – in Fäden über das Dessert gezogen – und Walnusskernen garnieren.

Tipp Sie können das Rezept beliebig umwandeln. Nehmen Sie z. B. statt der Zitronen 300 g Himbeeren (frisch oder tiefgefroren) und rühren Sie unter das Ganze zusätzlich einen guten Schuss Mandelsirup. Mit Kakaopulver und ein paar übrig gebliebenen Himbeeren garnieren.

LEMON CREAM

Preparation time about 10 minutes + 1 hour cooling time

When I was a little girl, there was nothing better than the lemon cream my grandmother used to make for me. Unfortunately, grandma died many years ago and I had failed to ask her for the recipe before she passed away. It took several attempts to create the true cream, but I am satisfied with the end result – and my grandma in heaven would be, too. The following recipe portion serves 8 people or a double serving is enough for 4 people.

INGREDIENTS

1 cup mascarpone
2 cups low-fat curd cheese
scant 1 cup cream
5 sachets vanilla sugar
2 Tb sugar
approx. 1/2 cup milk
juice of 3 lemons, according to taste
grated rind of 1 untreated lemon

TO GARNISH 1 lime or alternatively 1 lemon, sliced, honey, 1 Tb chopped walnuts

METHOD

Add all the ingredients for the cream one after another (the lemon cream in a glass bowl looks very pretty) in a large bowl and mix into a smooth consistency. Finally stir in lemon juice and lemon rind abrasion. Possibly with sugar to taste.
Refrigerate the cream for about 60 minutes. Garnish serving with lime slices, honey – laced-through the dessert – and walnuts.

Tip & Hints You can freely alter the recipe. For example, instead of the lemon you can stir in 3 cups raspberries (fresh or frozen) and in addition, a good shot of almond syrup. Garnish with cocoa powder and a few remaining raspberries.

Extras

HOLLERSIRUP

Zubereitungszeit 10 Minuten + insgesamt 4 Tage Ruhezeit

Holunder, umgangssprachlich Holler, gilt in der bäuerlichen Tradition Bayerns als Heilmittel. Die Blätter dieses Strauches werden kopfschmerzgeplagten Menschen zur Linderung auf die Stirn gelegt. Der Strauch an sich, nahe ans Haus gepflanzt, bildet einem alten Glauben nach einen sicheren Schutz gegen Blitzschlag. Und sogar gegen Hexen und Dämonen soll er seine Äste abwehrend in den Himmel halten können. Sein Sirup, hergestellt aus den Blütendolden, hat bestimmt auch irgendeine heilende Wirkung, die mir nicht bekannt sind, erfrischt aber in erster Linie, vermengt mit kühlem Wasser, Körper und Geist an heißen Sommertagen.

ZUTATEN

12–14 Hollerblütendolden, gewaschen und vorsichtig trocken getupft
3 unbehandelte Zitronen, in dicke Scheiben geschnitten
3 l Wasser
3 kg Zucker
50 g Zitronensäure (finden Sie in der Backabteilung eines gut sortierten Lebensmittelladens und in Apotheken)

AUSSERDEM 1 große Schüssel, Geschirrtuch zum Abdecken, 1 großer Topf mit Deckel, verschließbare Flaschen oder Gläser zum Abfüllen

ZUBEREITUNG

Hollerblütendolden mit den Zitronenscheiben in eine große Schüssel mit Wasser geben und das Gefäß abdecken. Das Ganze 3 Tage an einem kühlen und trockenen Ort ziehen lassen. Dann die Flüssigkeit in einen großen Topf abseihen, Zucker zugeben und aufkochen lassen. Vom Herd nehmen und abkühlen lassen. Anschließend mit einem Deckel abdecken und den Topf einen weiteren Tag (bzw. über Nacht) stehen lassen. Zum Schluss Zitronensäure zugeben und gut unterrühren.
Den Sirup in Flaschen oder Gläser füllen und kühl lagern. Hollersirup hält sich über viele Monate hinweg.

Tipp Geben Sie einen Schuss Hollersirup und ein paar tiefgefrorene Himbeeren – oder leicht gestampfte Erdbeeren – in ein Glas und füllen Sie das Ganze mit Prosecco auf. Ein Minzblatt rundet diesen leckeren Aperitif ab.

ELDERFLOWER SYRUP

Preparation time 10 minutes + 4 days to set

Elder ("Holunder"), which are called "Holler" in colloquial German, have traditionally been believed to have healing powers. The leaves of the bush are laid across the forehead of those who suffer from headaches. The bush in and of itself, was thought to protect your house from lightning when it was planted near the house. It was even supposed to ward off demons and witches. The syrup, which is made from the blossoms of the elderberry bush, probably has some healing properties I don't know about as well, but above all, it is a refreshment for body and soul when thinned with cold water on hot summer days.

INGREDIENTS

12–14 elderberry bush umbels, carefully washed and dried
3 untreated lemons, cut in thick slices
12 1/2 cups water
scant 4 1/2 cups sugar
5 Tb citric acid (can be found in the baking goods lane in a well-stocked grocery store or in pharmacies)

IN ADDITION 1 large bowl, kitchen towel for covering, 1 large lidded pot, sealable bottles or jars for storage

METHOD

Put the elderberry umbels and the lemon slices together in a large bowl with water; cover and let sit in a cool place for 3 whole days. Strain the liquid into a pot, add the sugar and let it come to a boil. Remove from heat and let cool. Cover the pot with a lid and let sit for another day or just overnight. Lastly, add the citric acid as a preservative and stir well.
The syrup should be filled into bottles or jars and will keep for several months when kept in a cool place.

Tips & Hints Add a dash of the syrup and a few frozen raspberries – or fresh strawberries, if possible – to your glass of bubbly. A mint leaf perfectly rounds off this delicious aperitif.

EIERLIKÖR

Zubereitungszeit ca. 20 Minuten + 1 Stunde Kühlzeit

Eierlikör ist ja nun eigentlich kein klassisch bayerisches Getränk, da kommt einem wohl eher ein kühles Bier in den Sinn. Und auch in Sachen Digestif denkt man im südlichsten Freistaat Deutschlands eher an einen herzhaft klaren Schnaps. Aber der Bayer an sich schätzt zuweilen durchaus auch ein süßes Likörchen, vor allem als Dessertzugabe. Danach kann man sich ja immer noch ein Stamperl Williamsbirne oder selbst gebrannten Kirschgeist genehmigen.

ZUTATEN

6 sehr frische Eigelb
175 g Puderzucker
2 TL (1 Pck.) Vanillezucker
375 ml Whiskey
375 g Sahne

AUSSERDEM Trichter, Flasche mit Verschluss zum Abfüllen

ZUBEREITUNG

Eigelbe in einer Schüssel zusammen mit Puderzucker und Vanillezucker schaumig schlagen. Whiskey nach und nach langsam zugeben, dabei die Schaummasse ununterbrochen weiter schlagen. Zum Schluss die Sahne unter ständigem Rühren zugeben.

Den Eierlikör zugedeckt im Kühlschrank ca. 1 Stunde ruhen lassen, dann mithilfe eines Trichters abfüllen und gut verschließen. Der Eierlikör ist 2–3 Wochen im Kühlschrank haltbar.

EGG LIQUEUR

Preparation time approx. 20 minutes + 1 hour to cool and set

Eggnog isn't exactly the first thing that comes to mind when you think of a classic Bavarian drink – that would be a cold beer. Even when a Bavarian thinks of a digestive or cordial, a clear hard liquor is what would come to mind, even though they truly do appreciate the sweet liqueur, especially as an accompaniment to their dessert. After that, you can always still toss down a fruit schnapps or have a shot of a home-made cherry schnapps.

INGREDIENTS

6 very fresh egg yolks
1 1/3 cups powdered sugar
2 tsp (1sachet) vanilla sugar
1 1/2 cups whiskey
1 1/2 cups cream

IN ADDITION funnel, lidded bottle for storage

METHOD

Whisk egg yolks, powdered sugar and vanilla sugar in a bowl until foamy. Slowly and gradually add the whiskey without stopping to beat the foamy mixture. Continue to stir and slowly add the cream.

Refrigerate the egg liqueur for approximately 1 hour. Then pour into the lidded bottle using a funnel and seal tightly. If kept in the refrigerator, the egg liqueur will keep for 2–3 weeks.

Weihnachtsbäckerei

Christmas Treats

In Bayern wird die Adventszeit auch »staade Zeit«, also »stille Zeit« genannt. Sie ist vollgepackt mit uralten überlieferten Ritualen und Mythen, die teilweise noch aus vorchristlicher Zeit stammen. Wussten Sie, dass beispielsweise die Form der Zimtsterne einen heidnischen Ursprung hat? Die Sterne beziehen sich nämlich nicht auf den berühmten Stern am Himmel, der einst die Geburtsstätte des Jesuskindes anzeigte, sondern sie symbolisieren Licht und Wärme und sollen die Menschen daran erinnern, dass mit der Wintersonnwende am 21. Dezember die Tage wieder länger werden und die Dunkelheit ein Ende nimmt.
Der 24. Dezember galt in früheren Zeiten als strenger Fastentag, an dem grundsätzlich nur Dörrobst zu sich genommen wurde, und auch heute kommt in vielen bayerischen Familien der eigentliche Festschmaus erst am 1. Weihnachtsfeiertag auf den Tisch. Dafür dürfen die Geschenke bereits in der Heiligen Nacht ausgepackt werden.

In Bavaria, the advent season is also called "quiet time." It is packed with ancient traditional rituals and myths that originate from pre-Christian times to some extent. Did you know that, for example, the star-shaped cinnamon cookies have a pagan origin? The star does not refer to the star in the sky, which once appeared over the birthplace of Jesus, but rather symbolize light and heat, and to remind people that with the winter solstice on December 21, the days will get longer and the darkness come to an end.
The 24th December was considered in the past as a strict fast day, on which only dried fruit was eaten, and even today the real feast is served in many Bavarian families on the first day of Christmas. The gifts can be opened on this holy night.

BRATÄPFEL

Zubereitungszeit inkl. Garzeit ca. 30–40 Minuten

ZUTATEN

4 TL Johannisbeergelee oder wahlweise Aprikosenmarmelade oder Zwetschgenmus
ca. 50 g Mandelsplitter oder Mandelblättchen
1 EL Rosinen
1 Prise Zimt
4 mittelgroße Boskopäpfel, gewaschen und mit einem Apfelstecher vom Kerngehäuse befreit
ca. 50 g zerlassene Butter

AUSSERDEM Butter zum Einfetten der Auflaufform

ZUBEREITUNG

Backrohr auf 200 Grad vorheizen.
Johannisbeergelee, Mandeln, Rosinen und Zimt in einer Schüssel miteinander verrühren. Anschließend die Äpfel mit der Masse füllen. Äpfel mit der zerlassenen Butter bepinseln und in die eingefettete Auflaufform setzen. Ca. 25 Minuten im Ofen garen. Heiß servieren!

BAKED APPLES

Preparation time including cooking time 30–40 minutes

INGREDIENTS

4 tsp currant jelly or either apricot jam or plum purée
approx. 1/4 cup almond slices or almond flakes
1 Tb raisins
1 pinch cinnamon
4 medium-sized Boskop apples, washed and freed from the cores with an apple corer
approx. 3 Tb melted butter

IN ADDITION butter for greasing the baking dish

METHOD

Preheat the oven to 400°F.
Mix the currant jelly, almonds, raisins, and cinnamon together in a bowl. Then fill the apples with the mixture. Brush apples with melted butter and place in the greased casserole dish. Cook for about 25 minutes in the oven. Serve hot.

Tipp Sie können anstatt des Johannisbeergelees oder einer anderen Konfitüre auch 100 g Marzipanrohmasse verwenden. Oder Sie füllen Ihre Äpfel mit einem Gemisch aus Honig und Mandeln.

Tips & Hints You can use also 3 1/2 oz of raw marzipan instead of currant jelly or a different jam. Or fill your apples with a mixture of honey and almonds.

CHRISTSTOLLEN

Ergibt 1 Stollen
Zubereitungszeit ca. 20 Minuten + Gehzeit insgesamt 1,5 Stunden + Backzeit ca. 45–50 Minuten + mindestens 3 Wochen Ruhezeit

Der Christstollen ist in ganz Deutschland beliebt. Sachsens Landeshauptstadt Dresden sowie das mittelfränkische Nürnberg sind für ihre leckeren Stollen sogar weltweit bekannt. Die Form des Stollens soll übrigens an das in Tücher gewickelte Jesuskind in der Krippe erinnern.
Der fertig gebackene Christstollen sollte wochenlang ruhen, damit er sein volles Aroma entwickeln kann. Backen Sie Ihren Stollen also am besten zu Beginn der Adventszeit, damit er rechtzeitig zu Weihnachten serviert werden kann.

ZUTATEN

FÜR DEN VORTEIG
20 g frische Hefe
1 Prise Zucker
1–2 EL Mehl
2–3 EL lauwarmes Wasser

FÜR DEN TEIG
300 g Mehl
100 g Butter, zimmerwarm
1/8 l lauwarme Milch
80 g Zucker
Abrieb von 1 unbehandelten Zitrone
1–2 Tropfen Bittermandelaroma
Mark von 1/2 Vanilleschote
1 Msp. gemahlener Kardamom
1 Prise Muskat
50 g Orangeat, gewürfelt
50 g Zitronat, gewürfelt
100 g gehackte Mandeln, wahlweise gemahlen
200 g Rosinen
nach Belieben 20 ml Rum
1 Prise Salz

AUSSERDEM Nudelholz, 1 Backblech, Backpapier, ca. 60 g zerlassene Butter zum Bestreichen des Stollens, 2 TL (1 Pck.) Vanillezucker und reichlich Puderzucker zum Bestreuen

CHRISTMAS CAKE

Yields 1 cake
Preparation time 20 minutes + resting time 1.5 hours total + baking time 45–50 minutes + at least 3 weeks rest period

This cake is popular all over Germany. Saxony State capital Dresden and the Middle Franconian Nuremberg are world-known for their delicious Christmas cakes. The shape of the elongated oval loaf is vaguely reminiscent of Jesus wrapped in blankets in the crib.
The finished cake should rest for weeks so that it can develop its optimum flavor. It is best to bake your cakes at the beginning of the advent season so that they can be served in time for Christmas.

INGREDIENTS

FOR THE YEAST STARTER
7/10 oz fresh yeast
1 pinch sugar
1–2 Tb flour
2–3 Tb lukewarm water

FOR THE DOUGH
2 2/5 cups flour
7 Tb butter at room temperature
1/2 cup lukewarm milk
1/3 cup sugar
grated rind of 1 untreated lemon
1–2 drops of bitter almond aroma
pulp of 1/2 vanilla pod
1 pinch ground cardamom
1 pinch nutmeg
2 oz candied orange peel, diced
2 oz candied lemon peel, diced
1 cup chopped or ground almonds
7 oz raisins
4 tsp rum to taste
1 pinch salt

IN ADDITION rolling pin, 1 baking sheet, baking paper, approx. 4 Tb melted butter for brushing the cake, 2 tsp (1 sachet) vanilla sugar and plenty of powdered sugar for sprinkling

ZUBEREITUNG

Alle Zutaten für den Vorteig in einer kleinen Schüssel gut miteinander verrühren und an einem warmen, nicht zugigen Ort zugedeckt 15 Minuten gehen lassen.

Mehl in eine große Schüssel sieben, eine Mulde in das Mehl drücken und den Vorteig einfüllen. Butter und Milch zugeben und mit den Knethaken Ihres Rührgeräts – oder mit den Händen – alles locker miteinander verkneten. Dann der Reihe nach die weiteren Zutaten zugeben und zu einem geschmeidigen, glänzenden Teig verarbeiten. Den Stollenteig zugedeckt wieder am selben Ort 45 Minuten leicht aufgehen lassen.

Anschließend den Teig noch einmal gut durchkneten und anschließend ca. 1 cm dick ausrollen. Zunächst die eine Seite des Teigs bis zur Mitte hin einschlagen, dann die andere, sodass die beiden sich leicht überlappen. Den Stollen auf das vorbereitete Backblech legen und noch einmal 30 Minuten zugedeckt ruhen lassen. Backofen auf 200 Grad vorheizen.

Den Christstollen in ca. 45–50 Minuten goldbraun backen. Stäbchenprobe machen!

Den noch warmen Stollen mit zerlassener Butter bestreichen. Lassen Sie die Butter immer wieder einziehen, bevor Sie erneut über die Oberfläche pinseln. Vanillezucker gleichmäßig darüberstreuen.

Vollkommen auskühlen lassen und erst dann mit Puderzucker bestreuen, sonst bekommt Ihr Stollen einen unansehnlichen Gelbstich. Geizen Sie nicht mit dem Puderzucker, schließlich erinnert die dicke Schicht an frisch gefallenen Schnee.

Den Stollen einen Tag lang zugedeckt ruhen lassen, dann fest in Frischhaltefolie wickeln und an einem trockenen Ort mindestens 3 Wochen lang durchziehen lassen.

METHOD

Mix all the ingredients for the yeast starter together in a small bowl and leave it in a warm, draft-free place covered for 15 minutes.

Sift flour into a large bowl, press a hollow in the flour and pour in the yeast starter. Using the dough hook on your mixer, – or your hands – mix the butter and milk together and loosely knead everything. Then add the other ingredients and process to a smooth, shiny dough. Cover and leave in a warm, draft-free place for 45 minutes.

Then knead the dough again and roll out to about 1/3 inch thick. First turn over one side of the dough to the middle, then turn over the other side, so that they overlap slightly in the middle. Place the cake on the prepared baking sheet and leave it covered to rest for 30 minutes again. Preheat the oven to 400°F.

Bake the cakes 45–50 minutes until golden brown. Skewer test.

Spread the warm melted butter on the cake. Make sure butter has soaked in before adding more. Sprinkle with vanilla sugar.

Allow to cool completely before sprinkling with powdered sugar, otherwise your cake will develop an unsightly yellow tinge. Don't skimp with the powdered sugar; it resembles the thick layer of freshly fallen snow.

Let the elongated oval loaf rest for a day, then tightly wrap in plastic wrap, leave in a dry place for at least 3 weeks.

KLETZENBROT

Zubereitungszeit ca. 45 Minuten + Einweichzeit für die Trockenfrüchte 12 Stunden + Gehzeit insgesamt 1 Stunde + Backzeit ca. 45–60 Minuten

In früheren Zeiten war es selbstverständlich, dass man sich auf den bäuerlichen Höfen Bayerns das Brot für den täglichen Bedarf selbst backte. Dafür gab es zuweilen extragroße Brotbacköfen, die außerhalb des Hauses standen und die richtig gut befeuert werden mussten, um eine ordentliche Glut zu produzieren. Nicht selten trafen sich an solch einem Backtag mehrere Nachbarinnen von den umliegenden Höfen, und gemeinsam backte man den Bedarf für alle Familien für die nächsten Tage und Wochen.
Zur Adventszeit ergänzte die Hausfrau dann ihren Brotteig mit Nüssen und getrockneten Früchten wie Birnen, Zwetschgen, Feigen, Aprikosen und Äpfeln – daher auch der ungewöhnliche Name dieses Brotes, denn »Kletzen« ist das umgangssprachliche Wort für getrocknete Birnen. Übrigens gibt es sogar einen festen »Kletzenbrotbacktag« im bayerischen Brauchtumskalender: die Wintersonnwende, der 21. Dezember. Zum Verzehr angeschnitten wird das Kletzenbrot traditionell erst nach Weihnachten, nämlich am 26.12.

Für nachstehendes Rezept benötigen Sie also frischen Brotteig, am besten aus einem Roggenmehlgemisch. Vielleicht ist Ihr Bäcker um die Ecke so nett und verkauft Ihnen ein bisschen von seinem Teig, aber im Grunde ist er sehr leicht selbst herzustellen, wie Sie im Folgenden sehen können.

ZUTATEN

FÜR DIE FÜLLUNG

100 g Kletzen (getrocknete Birnen)
100 g Dörrpflaumen
50 g getrocknete Feigen
50 g getrocknete Aprikosen
50 g getrocknete Apfelringe
60 ml Rum
100 g Walnüsse
50 g geschälte Mandeln
50 g Orangeat
50 g Zitronat
100 g Zucker
1 TL Zimt
1 Msp. Nelkenpulver
1 Msp. Muskat

BREAD FROM DRIED PEARS

Preparation time approx. 45 minutes + soaking time for the dried fruit 12 hours + resting time total 1 hour + baking time 45–60 minutes

In the past, at the peasant farms in Bavaria, bread was baked daily. Sometimes there were extra-large bread ovens, which were outside the house and the wood for these needed to be burnt to produce a neat glow. It was common for neighboring farmers to come gather on these days and bake what they need for all their families for the next few days and weeks together. During advent, the housewives then added nuts and dried fruits such as pears, plums, figs, apricots and apples to their bread – hence the unusual name of this bread, because "Kletzen" is the colloquial word for dried pears. Incidentally, there is even a fixed "bread from dried pears day" in the Bavarian tradition calendar: the winter solstice, December 21. Intended for human consumption, we cut the bread from dried pears traditionally only after Christmas, namely the 26th of December.

The following recipe requires fresh bread dough; the best is from a mixture of rye flour. Perhaps your bakery around the corner would be so generous as to sell you a little bit of their starter dough, but in fact it is very easy to make as you can see in the following.

INGREDIENTS

FOR THE FILLING

3 1/2 oz Kletzen (dried pears)
3 1/2 oz dried plums
2 oz dried figs
2 oz dried apricots
2 oz dried apple rings
4 Tb rum
1 cup walnuts
1/3 cup peeled almonds
7/10 oz candied orange peel
7/10 oz candied lemon peel
1/2 cup sugar
1 tsp cinnamon
1 pinch clove powder
1 pinch nutmeg powder

FOR THE DOUGH

3 cups rye flour type 1150
2 cups whole wheat flour

FÜR DEN TEIG

250 g Roggenmehl, Type 1150
250 g Weizenvollkornmehl
1,5 Pck. Trockenhefe
2 EL herber Honig, wie z. B. Kastanien-, Berg- oder Tannenhonig
1 TL Salz
500 g Kefir, lauwarm erhitzt
50 g zerlassene Butter

AUSSERDEM Backpapier, Backblech

ZUBEREITUNG

Am Vortag des Kletzenbrotbacktages alle Trockenfrüchte in warmes Wasser geben und über Nacht einweichen lassen.
Am nächsten Tag ca. 10 EL des Einweichwassers beiseitenehmen, dann die Früchte abgießen und klein schneiden – Stiele und Kerne gegebenenfalls entfernen. In eine Schüssel geben und mit Rum vermengen.
Walnüsse, Mandeln, Orangeat und Zitronat hacken und in einer separaten Schüssel mit Zucker, Zimt, Nelkenpulver und Muskat vermischen.
Für den Brotteig die beiden Mehlsorten mit der Trockenhefe vermischen. Dann Honig, Trockenfrüchte, das Nuss-Zitrusfrucht-Gemisch und 1 TL Salz untermengen und gut miteinander verkneten. Lauwarmen Kefir und Butter in den Teig arbeiten und das Ganze dann zugedeckt an einem warmen, nicht zugigen Ort 30 Minuten gehen lassen. Dann den Teig nochmals gut durchkneten und aus der Masse einen großen oder zwei kleine Laibe formen. Auf das vorbereitete Backblech legen und zugedeckt erneut 30 Minuten gehen lassen.
Backofen auf 200 Grad vorheizen und die Laibe dann in ca. 45–60 Minuten goldbraun backen. Noch warm mit der Einweichflüssigkeit bestreichen und dann auskühlen lassen.

Tipp *Kletzenbrot lässt sich gut einfrieren, bleibt aber auch so, in Frischhaltefolie eingewickelt, viele Tage lang frisch und saftig.*

1 1/2 packs of dry yeast
2 Tb sour honey or tart, such as chestnut, mountain, or pine
1 tsp salt
2 cups kefir, lukewarm heated
3 Tb melted butter

IN ADDITION baking paper, baking sheet

METHOD

On the eve of the baking day for "bread from dried pears," leave all dried fruits in warm water and soak overnight.
The next day take aside approximately 10 Tb of the soaking water, then drain the fruits and cut into small pieces, removing, if necessary, any stalks and seeds. Mix in a bowl with rum.
Chop walnuts, almonds, candied orange peel and candied lemon peel and mix with sugar, cinnamon, cloves, and nutmeg in a separate bowl.
Mix the two types of flour with the dry yeast for the bread dough. Then mix honey, dried fruit, nut-fruit mixture and 1 tsp salt and knead together. Work lukewarm kefir and butter into the dough and then cover the whole thing on a warm, draft-free place for 30 minutes. Then again knead the dough well and form a large or two small loaves from the mixture. Place on the prepared baking sheet and cover and leave again for 30 minutes.
Preheat the oven to 400°F and bake the loaves for 45–60 minutes until golden brown. While still warm, coat with the soaking liquid and then allow to cool.

Tips & Hints *Bread from dried pears can be frozen, and even remains fresh and juicy when wrapped in plastic wrap for many days.*

LEBKUCHEN

Ergibt ca. 60 Stück
Zubereitungszeit inkl. Backzeit ca. 45 Minuten + mindestens 2 Stunden Kühlzeit für den Teig + mindestens 12 Stunden (über Nacht) Ruhezeit für die Lebkuchenrohlinge

Lebkuchen sind für viele Menschen der Inbegriff von Weihnachten und der vorangehenden Adventszeit, und sie erfreuen sich nicht nur in Bayern großer Beliebtheit. Sie sind leicht zuzubereiten und lassen sich wunderbar weiterverarbeiten (s. Lebkuchenstrudel S. 36). So manch findiger bayerischer Koch schwört sogar auf altbackene Lebkuchen in der Soße für seinen Schweinebraten, doch das ist eine andere Geschichte.

GINGERBREAD

Yields approx. 60 pieces
Preparation time including baking time 45 minutes + at least 2 hours cooling time for the dough + at least 12 hours (overnight) resting period for the gingerbread

For so many people, gingerbread is the epitome of Christmas and the preceding advent season; in Bavaria eating gingerbread is very popular. It is easy to make and wonderful to serve (see gingerbread swirl pg. 36). Even some resourceful Bavarian chefs swear by stale gingerbread in the sauce for their roasted pork, but that's a different story.

ZUTATEN

4 Eier
300 g Muscovadozucker
2 TL (1 Pck.) Vanillezucker
1 Prise Salz
3 EL Mehl
3 EL Speisestärke
2 EL Kakaopulver
1–2 EL Lebkuchengewürz
1 EL Rum
ca. 80 g Zitronat, wahlweise Orangeat, fein gehackt
100 g gemahlene Haselnüsse
200 g gemahlene Mandeln

AUSSERDEM Backoblaten, 50 mm Durchmesser, 2–3 Backbleche, Backpapier

ZUBEREITUNG

Eier in eine Schüssel geben und zusammen mit Muscovado- und Vanillezucker schaumig rühren. Eine Prise Salz zugeben. Dann nach und nach alle anderen Zutaten zugeben und gut miteinander verrühren. Den Teig abschmecken, um die passende Menge Lebkuchengewürz festzustellen. Die Schüssel abdecken und für mindestens 2 Stunden – am besten jedoch über Nacht – in den Kühlschrank stellen.
Den Teig in sehr großzügigen Häufchen auf den Oblaten verteilen. Nehmen Sie dazu einen Teelöffel und zusätzlich Ihre sauberen Hände zu Hilfe. Der Teig ist recht klebrig, sodass sie ihn mit den Fingern vielleicht etwas zurechtstreichen müssen. Achten Sie darauf, die Lebkuchenrohlinge nicht zu dicht nebeneinander auf das Blech zu setzen, der Teig läuft beim Backen noch ziemlich auseinander.
Die Lebkuchenrohlinge über Nacht bei Zimmertemperatur ruhen lassen.
Am nächsten Tag das Backrohr auf 225 Grad vorheizen und die Lebkuchen im Ofen 4–5 Minuten backen. Anschließend gut auskühlen lassen.

Tipps

* *Die lange Ruhezeit der Lebkuchenrohlinge über Nacht bewirkt, dass die fertigen Lebkuchen länger weich und saftig bleiben. Sie halten sich in gut verschließbaren Vorratsdosen, an einem kühlen Ort gelagert, mehrere Wochen lang.*
* *Der Abrieb einer unbehandelten Orange gibt Ihrem Lebkuchenteig mehr Frische.*

INGREDIENTS

4 eggs
1 1/2 cups muscovado sugar
2 tsp (1 sachet) vanilla sugar
1 pinch salt
3 Tb flour
3 Tb starch
2 Tb cocoa powder
1–2 Tb gingerbread spice
1 Tb rum
approx. 3 oz candied lemon peel, optional candied orange peel, finely chopped
1 cup ground hazelnuts
2 cups ground almonds

IN ADDITION baking wafers, diameter 2 inches, 2–3 baking trays, baking paper

METHOD

Mix the eggs in a bowl with muscovado and vanilla sugar until foamy. Add a pinch of salt. Then add all the other ingredients and mix well together. To enhance the taste of the dough, add the appropriate amount of gingerbread spice. Cover the bowl and leave for at least 2 hours – best however is overnight – in the refrigerator.
Distribute the dough in very generous mounds on the wafers. Take a teaspoon for this and in addition your hands. The dough is quite sticky, so you may need to gently spread it across the baking wafers with your fingers. Be sure not to put the gingerbread too close together on the tray, as the dough can spread while baking.
Leave the gingerbread overnight at room temperature.
The next day, preheat the oven to 450°F and bake the gingerbread in the oven for 4–5 minutes. Then allow to cool.

Tips & Hints

* *That long break, a kind of "relaxation" period for the gingerbread overnight causes it to stay soft and juicy longer. You can store these breads in a cool place for several weeks, in a good sealable storage box.*
* *You can refine your gingerbread dough: In addition, the grated rind of an untreated orange can give it more freshness.*

HASELNUSSPLÄTZCHEN

Zubereitungszeit inkl. Backzeit ca. 1,5 Stunden + mindestens 2 Stunden Kühlzeit für den Teig

ZUTATEN

175 g Mehl
200 g gemahlene Haselnüsse
175 g Zucker
2 TL (1 Pck.) Vanillezucker
175 g kalte Butter
Abrieb von 1 unbehandelten Orange

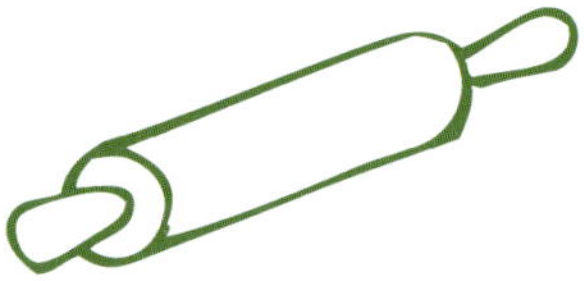

AUSSERDEM Frischhaltefolie, 150 g Vollmilchkuvertüre, wahlweise auch dunkle Kuvertüre, je nach Geschmack, 50–100 g ganze Haselnüsse, Backblech, Backpapier

ZUBEREITUNG

Alle Zutaten rasch zu einem Teig kneten. Nicht zu lange kneten, sonst wird er bröselig, aber darauf achten, dass die Butter gut verknetet ist. Den Teig in zwei gleich große Teile teilen und zwei Stränge mit einem Durchmesser von 3–4 cm daraus formen. Die Stränge einzeln in Frischhaltefolie wickeln und für mindestens 2 Stunden – am besten jedoch über Nacht – in den Kühlschrank legen.
Backofen auf 180 Grad vorheizen. Backblech mit Backpapier auslegen. Den ersten Teigstrang in ca. 3 mm dicke Scheiben schneiden und die Scheiben aufs Blech legen. Ca. 15 Minuten goldgelb backen. Den übrigen Teig so lange wieder im Kühlschrank zwischenlagern, bis Sie ihn benötigen. Mit dem zweiten Teigstrang ebenso verfahren.
Nebenher die Kuvertüre im Wasserbad erhitzen und auf die noch heißen Plätzchen pinseln. Mit jeweils einer ganzen Haselnuss dekorieren – die klebt am besten, wenn Sie einen Extraklecks Kuvertüre in die Mitte des Plätzchens setzen, mit dem Sie die Nuss »festkleben«.

Tipp Sie können die Plätzchen auch mit Marmelade oder Konfitüre Ihrer Wahl füllen. Sehr gut passen säuerliche oder leicht bittere Fruchtaufstriche wie Sauerkirschkonfitüre oder Orangenmarmelade. Dazu jeweils einen Klecks Marmelade in die Mitte eines Plätzchens geben und mit einem zweiten Plätzchen abdecken und leicht andrücken. Anschließend mit Kuvertüre und Haselnüssen wie oben verfahren.

HAZELNUT COOKIES

Preparation time including baking time approx. 1.5 hours + 2 hours cooling time for the dough

INGREDIENTS

1 1/2 cups flour
2 cups ground hazelnuts
1 cup sugar
2 tsp (1 sachet) vanilla sugar
12 Tb cold butter
grated rind of 1 untreated orange

IN ADDITION clear plastic wrap, 1/3 lb milk couverture, either dark chocolate, depending on taste, 2–4 oz whole hazelnuts, baking sheet, baking paper

METHOD

Knead all ingredients quickly into a dough. Not too long kneading, otherwise the surface will get crumbly, but make sure the butter is well mixed. Divide the dough into two equal parts and form two lines with a diameter of 1.5 inches from it. Wrap the strands individually in plastic wrap and leave for at least 2 hours – best however overnight – in the refrigerator.
Preheat the oven to 350°F. Line baking sheet with parchment paper. Cut the first strand of dough into approx. 1/10 inches thick slices and lay the slices on the plate. Bake for 15 minutes until golden. Leave the remaining dough wrapped in cling film in the refrigerator. Repeat with the second strand.
At the same time heat the chocolate in a bain-marie and brush it on the still hot cookie. Decorate each with a whole hazelnut – it sticks best if you put an extra dollop of couverture in the center of the cookie.

Tips & Hints You can fill the cookies with jam or preserves of your choice. Tart or slightly bitter fruit spreads like sour cherry jam or orange marmalade fit very well with the hazelnut cookies. Add a dab of jam in the middle of a cookie and cover with a second cookie and gently press. Then proceed with chocolate and hazelnuts as above.

HUSARENKNÖPFERL

Zubereitungszeit inkl. Backzeit ca. 75 Minuten + mindestens 2 Stunden Kühlzeit für den Teig

ZUTATEN

FÜR DEN TEIG

200 g Mehl
2 TL (1 Pck.) Vanillezucker
40 g Zucker
125 g kalte Butter
2 Eigelb
1 TL Orangenmehl (getrocknete und anschließend fein gemörserte Orangenschale; Herstellung s. *Tipps*)

ZUM FÜLLEN

Himbeerkonfitüre, Johannisbeergelee oder Aprikosenkonfitüre

AUSSERDEM Frischhaltefolie, Backpapier, Backblech, Mehl zum Bestäuben der Arbeitsfläche, 1 kleiner Holzkochlöffel

ZUBEREITUNG

Aus den Zutaten für den Teig eine glatte Teigkugel kneten (nicht zu lange kneten, damit der Teig nicht zu weich wird). Die Teigkugel in Folie schlagen und für mindestens 2 Stunden – am besten jedoch über Nacht – in den Kühlschrank legen.
Anschließend den Backofen auf 180 Grad vorheizen. Das Backblech mit Backpapier auslegen. Die Arbeitsfläche dünn mit Mehl bestäuben. Die Teigkugel in ca. 1 cm dicke Scheiben schneiden und einzeln zu 1 cm dicken Strängen rollen. Teig, den Sie gerade nicht benötigen, wieder in die Frischhaltefolie einwickeln und in den Kühlschrank legen.
Die Teigstränge in kleine Stücke schneiden und etwa daumennagelgroße Kügelchen daraus formen. Die Kügelchen auf das Backblech legen und mit dem Stielende des Kochlöffels kleine Mulden in die Mitte der einzelnen Husarenknöpferl drücken. Die Mulden mit der Marmelade Ihrer Wahl füllen. Ins Backrohr schieben und ca. 10–15 Minuten goldgelb backen. So verfahren, bis der Teig aufgebraucht ist.

HUSAR BUTTONS

(JAM-FILLED BUTTER COOKIES)

Preparation time including baking time approx. 75 minutes + at least 2 hours cooling time

INGREDIENTS

FOR THE DOUGH

1 3/5 cups flour
2 tsp (1 sachet) vanilla sugar
1 1/2 Tb sugar
8 Tb cold butter
2 egg yolks
1 tsp orange powder (dried and finely ground orange peel; s. *Tips & Hints*)

FOR THE FILLING

raspberry jam, currant jelly or apricot jam

IN ADDITION clear plastic wrap, baking sheet, baking paper, flour for dusting the work surface, 1 small wooden spoon

METHOD

Knead the ingredients into a smooth, firm dough (make sure not to knead too long so that dough does not become too soft). Wrap the dough in clear plastic wrap and refrigerate for at least 2 hours – if possible overnight.
Preheat oven to 350°F; line the baking sheet with baking parchment and dust the work surface with flour. Cut off 3/8-inch thick slices from the dough and shape each slice into 3/8-inch thick strips. Wrap and return any unused dough to the refrigerator.
Now cut the strips into small pieces, about the size of your thumbnail, and roll the pieces into balls. Place the balls of dough onto the baking sheet and with the handle of a wooden spoon make a small indentation in the center of the individual "buttons." Fill the buttons with a jam or jelly of your choice and bake for about 10–15 minutes until golden.
Continue this process with the remaining dough.

Tipps

* *Orangenmehl können Sie leicht selbst herstellen! Dazu die Schalen von 4–5 unbehandelten Orangen auf ein mit Backpapier ausgelegtes Backblech legen. Die weiße Innenhaut vorher vollständig entfernen. Für 3–4 Stunden bei 60 Grad auf mittlerer Schiene ins Backrohr schieben. Die trockenen Orangenschalen anschließend fein mörsern und das Orangenmehl in eine gut verschließbare Dose geben.*

Tips & Hints

* *You can make the orange powder yourself. Arrange the peels of 4–5 untreated oranges on a baking sheet laid out with parchment paper. Make sure there is no white residue on the inside of the orange peel. Bake for 3–4 hours on middle grate of oven at 140°F. Finely grind the dried peels using a mortar and then fill them into an airtight container.*

KOKOSMAKRONEN

Ergibt ca. 25 Stück
Zubereitungszeit inkl. Backzeit und Glasieren
ca. 1,5 Stunden

Kokosmakronen waren, als ich ein kleines Mädchen war, meine absoluten Lieblingsplätzchen! Ich war nahezu süchtig nach dieser weichen, saftigen Konsistenz und dem exotischen Kokosgeschmack. Leider öffnete meine Mutter die Plätzchendose immer erst kurz vor Weihnachten – dafür war die Freude dann umso größer!

ZUTATEN

- 4 Eiweiß
- 150 g Zucker
- 2 TL (1 Pck.) Vanillezucker
- 65 g Magerquark, 20% Fett i. Tr.
- 4 Tropfen Bittermandelaroma
- 200 g Kokosraspeln

AUSSERDEM Backoblaten, 50 mm Durchmesser, Backblech, Backpapier, dunkle Kuvertüre

ZUBEREITUNG

Eiweiße steif schlagen und beiseitestellen. Backofen auf 150 Grad vorheizen.
Die restlichen Zutaten miteinander vermischen, dann den Eischnee unterziehen. Je einen gehäuften Teelöffel Kokosmasse auf den Backoblaten verteilen. Die Kokosmakronen im Backofen ca. 20 Minuten lang sanft backen bzw. »trocknen lassen«. Die Makronen sind fertig, wenn die Oberflächen beginnen, sich gelblich zu verfärben; sie sollen keine goldbraune Färbung annehmen!
Kuvertüre im Wasserbad erhitzen und die ausgekühlten Kokosmakronen jeweils zur Hälfte mit der Schokolade bestreichen.

Tipp Für mehr Genuss einfach die Mengenangaben verdoppeln! Kokosmakronen halten sich in einer gut verschließbaren Vorratsdose, an einem kühlen Ort gelagert, mehrere Wochen lang.

COCONUT MACAROONS

Yields about 25 pieces
Preparation time including baking time and glazing
approx. 1.5 hours

Coconut macaroons were my absolute favorite cookies when I was a little girl. I was almost addicted to this soft, juicy texture and exotic coconut taste. Unfortunately, my mother always opened the cookie jar just before Christmas – that was an even greater joy for me.

INGREDIENTS

- 4 egg whites
- 2/3 cup sugar
- 2 tsp (1 sachet) vanilla sugar
- 1/4 cup low-fat curd cheese
- 4 drops bitter almond flavoring
- 3 cups grated coconut

IN ADDITION baking wafers, diameter 2 inches, baking sheet, baking paper, dark couverture

METHOD

Beat egg whites until stiff and set them aside. Preheat the oven to 300°F.
Mix the remaining ingredients together, then stir in the whipped egg whites. Spread a heaped teaspoon of the coconut mixture on the baking wafers. Bake the coconut macaroons in the oven for about 20 minutes gently or "dry." When the surfaces begin to turn a yellowish color, the macaroons are ready. They should not turn a golden brown color. Leave macaroons to cool.
Heat the chocolate in a bain-marie and spread over each half of the macaroons with the chocolate.

Tips & Hints Just double the quantities for more enjoyment. Coconut macaroons can be kept in a well-sealed storage container, stored in a cool place, for several weeks.

ORANGENPLÄTZCHEN

Zubereitungszeit inkl. Backzeit 1 Stunde 15 Minuten + mindestens 2 Stunden Kühlzeit

ZUTATEN

150 g Mehl
100 g Speisestärke
100 g Puderzucker
120 g kalte Butter
1 Ei
Abrieb von 1 unbehandelten Orange

AUSSERDEM Frischhaltefolie, 1 Plätzchenausstecher nach Wahl, Mehl für die Arbeitsfläche, Backblech, Backpapier, ca. 150 g Orangen- oder Blutorangenmarmelade, ca. 80–100 g dunkle Kuvertüre

ZUBEREITUNG

Alle Zutaten für den Teig zu einem festen Teig kneten und zu einem Ball formen. Die Teigkugel in Frischhaltefolie einwickeln und für mindestens 2 Stunden – am besten aber über Nacht – in den Kühlschrank legen.
Danach den Backofen auf 180 Grad vorheizen. Mehl dünn auf die Arbeitsfläche stäuben und eine dicke Scheibe vom Teigball schneiden. Den Rest wieder in Folie einpacken und im Kühlschrank zwischenlagern. Den Teig ca. 5 mm dick (nicht zu dünn!) ausrollen und ausstechen. Die Plätzchen ca. 15–20 Minuten im Ofen hellgelb backen. Auskühlen lassen.
So verfahren, bis der Teig aufgebraucht ist.
Kuvertüre im Wasserbad schmelzen. Währenddessen die Hälfte der Plätzchen mit Marmelade bestreichen und mit der anderen Hälfte abdecken, leicht andrücken. Die geschmolzene Kuvertüre auf die Plätzchen pinseln und erneut auskühlen lassen.

Tipps

* *In Zuckersirup gekochte Orangen- oder Zitronenzesten bilden einen wunderschönen farblichen Dekoabschluss auf Ihren Orangenplätzchen. Dazu 1 gehäuften EL Puderzucker in 2–3 EL Wasser aufkochen lassen. Zesten von 1 unbehandelten Orange oder 1 unbehandelten Zitrone zugeben und ca. 2–3 Minuten im Zuckerwasser köcheln lassen. Durch ein Sieb geben und die dünnen Zitrusfäden auf den dunklen Schokoladenoberflächen verteilen.*

ORANGE COOKIES

Preparation time including baking time 1 hour 15 minutes + at least 2 hours cooling time

INGREDIENTS

1 1/5 cups flour
1 cup starch
1/2 cup powdered sugar
8 Tb cold butter
1 egg
grated rind of 1 untreated orange

IN ADDITION clear platic wrap, 1 cookie cutter of your choice, flour for the work surface, baking sheet, baking paper, approx. 1/3 lb orange or blood orange marmalade, approx. 3–3 1/2 oz dark couverture

METHOD

Knead all the ingredients for the dough into a firm dough and shape into a ball. Wrap the ball of dough in plastic wrap and leave for at least 2 hours – for best results overnight – in the refrigerator.
Then preheat the oven to 350°F. Dust a thin layer of flour on the work surface and cut a thick slice from the dough ball. Leave the rest wrapped in foil in the refrigerator. Roll out the dough approx. 1/5 inches thick (not too thin) and cut out the dough. Bake the cookies for about 15–20 minutes in the oven until they turn a light yellow color. Allow to cool off.
Do this until the dough is used up.
Melt chocolate in a bain-marie. Meanwhile spread half of the cookies with jam, butter and cover it with the other half, press it lightly. Brush the melted chocolate over the cookie and let it cool again.

Tips & Hints

* *Decorate your cookie with a beautiful color, by making an orange juice or zest in sugar syrup mixture. Mix about 1 heaped Tb powdered sugar in 2–3 Tb boiling water. Add the zest of 1 untreated orange or lemon and simmer for 2–3 minutes in the sugar water. Sieve the mixture and spread the thin threads of citrus on the surface of the dark chocolate.*

SPITZBUBEN

Zubereitungszeit inkl. Backzeit ca. 90 Minuten + mindestens 2 Stunden Kühlzeit für den Teig

ZUTATEN

FÜR DEN TEIG

280 g Mehl
175 g kalte Butter
70 g Zucker
2 TL (1 Pck.) Vanillezucker
1 großes Ei

ZUM FÜLLEN

Johannisbeergelee

AUSSERDEM Frischhaltefolie, Mehl für die Arbeitsfläche, Backblech, Backpapier, rundes Ausstechförmchen, Puderzucker zum Bestäuben

ZUBEREITUNG

Aus den Zutaten für den Teig einen festen, glatten Plätzchenteig kneten, dabei darauf achten, dass der Teig nicht zu lange geknetet wird. Die fertige Teigkugel in Frischhaltefolie einschlagen und für mindestens 2 Stunden – besser noch über Nacht – in den Kühlschrank legen.

Backofen auf 180 Grad vorheizen. Teigkugel in ca. 1 cm dicke Scheiben schneiden und einzeln auf einer leicht bemehlten Arbeitsfläche messerrückendick ausrollen. Den gerade nicht benötigten Teig wieder in die Folie einwickeln und zurück in den Kühlschrank legen.

Backblech mit Backpapier auslegen. Die Plätzchen ausstechen und auf das Backblech legen. Im Ofen ca. 10–15 Minuten goldgelb backen. Zum Auskühlen auf einen Teller oder eine Platte geben. So verfahren, bis der gesamte Teig aufgebraucht ist.

Auf je eine Plätzchenunterseite einen Klecks Johannisbeergelee geben und mit einem zweiten Plätzchen bedecken. Leicht andrücken. Die Spitzbuben zum Schluss mit Puderzucker bestäuben.

Tipp Spitzbuben halten sich in gut verschließbaren Vorratsdosen, an einem kühlen Ort gelagert, mehrere Wochen lang.

LITTLE RASCALS

(BUTTER COOKIE SANDWICHES FILLED WITH CURRANT JELLY)

Preparation time including baking time approx. 90 minutes + at least 2 hours cooling time for the dough

INGREDIENTS

FOR THE DOUGH

2 cups flour
12 Tb cold butter
5 Tb sugar
2 tsp (1 sachet) vanilla sugar
1 large egg

FOR THE FILLING

red currant jelly

IN ADDITION clear plastic wrap, flour for dusting the work surface, baking sheet, baking parchment, round cookie cutout, powdered sugar for dusting

METHOD

Knead the ingredients into a firm, smooth dough, taking care not to knead too long. Wrap in clear plastic wrap and refrigerate for at least 2 hours – if possible overnight.

Preheat oven to 350°F. Now cut off 3/8-inch slices from the dough; roll out each slice on a clean, floured surface to 1/8 inch thick. Wrap and return any unused portion of the dough to the refrigerator.

Line the baking sheet with parchment. Now cut out cookies; place onto the baking sheet and bake for about 10–15 minutes until golden. Cool on either a plate or platter and continue the same process with the remaining dough.

Place a dollop of red currant jelly on the underside of one cookie and cover it with a second cookie, pressing lightly. Sprinkle the "Spitzbuben" with powdered sugar.

Tips & Hints "Spitzbuben" will keep for several weeks when kept in an airtight cookie jar or tin and stored in a cool place.

SPRITZGEBÄCK

Zubereitungszeit inkl. Backzeit ca. 1 Stunde 15 Minuten

ZUTATEN

250 g Butter, zimmerwarm
100 g Puderzucker
1 Ei, zimmerwarm
2 TL (1 Pck.) Vanillezucker
1 EL Kakaopulver
Abrieb von 1 unbehandelten Orange
300 g Mehl

AUSSERDEM Spritzbeutel mit großer Sterntülle, Backblech, Backpapier, nach Belieben ca. 100–150 g Konfitüre oder Marmelade nach Wahl zum Füllen, ca. 80 g Kuvertüre, wahlweise dunkle Schokolade oder Vollmilchschokolade

ZUBEREITUNG

Butter in eine Schüssel geben und cremig rühren. Puderzucker zugeben und unterrühren. Ei und Vanillezucker zugeben und die Masse schaumig schlagen. Dann Kakaopulver und Orangenabrieb zugeben und verrühren. Zum Schluss das Mehl dazusieben und am besten mit Knethaken einarbeiten, sodass ein zäher Rührteig entsteht.
Backofen auf 180 Grad vorheizen.
Den Teig portionsweise in den Spritzbeutel füllen – darauf achten, dass Sie den Beutel nicht zu voll machen, sonst wird es eine Sauerei, wie ich leidvoll feststellen musste – und auf das vorbereitete Backblech spritzen, sodass längliche, ca. 4 cm lange Stränge entstehen. Im Ofen ca. 12–14 Minuten backen. Abkühlen lassen. So verfahren, bis der Teig aufgebraucht ist.

Wenn Sie möchten, können Sie Ihr Spritzgebäck füllen, indem Sie jeweils ein Plätzchen mit Konfitüre bestreichen – am besten eignen sich leicht säuerliche Produkte, wie Johannisbeergelee, Orangen- oder Zitronenmarmelade –, um es dann mit einem zweiten Plätzchen abzudecken. Leicht andrücken und dann wie folgt mit der Kuvertüre fortfahren.

Für die Glasur Kuvertüre im Wasserbad erhitzen. Das gut ausgekühlte Gebäck mit einer Seite in die Kuvertüre tunken. Erneut auskühlen lassen.

SHORTCAKE BISCUITS

Preparation time including baking time 1 hour 15 minutes

INGREDIENTS

1/2 lb butter at room temperature
1 cup powdered sugar
1 egg at room temperature
2 tsp (1 sachet) vanilla sugar
1 Tb cocoa powder
grated rind of 1 untreated orange
2 2/5 cups flour

IN ADDITION icing pipe, baking sheet, baking paper, optional: about 3 1/2–5 1/3 oz marmalade or jam of your choice to fill, approx. 3 oz chocolate couverture, either dark chocolate or milk chocolate

METHOD

Mix butter in a bowl until creamy. Stir in the powdered sugar. Add egg and vanilla sugar and beat the mixture. Add cocoa powder and orange abrasion, then stir. Finally sift the flour. Mix using dough hooks as they produce a tougher batter.
Preheat the oven to 350°F.
Fill the dough portions in the icing pipe – make sure you do not fill the bag too much, otherwise it is a mess, as I discovered the hard way. Squirt on the prepared baking sheet, lengthwise, approximately 1 1/2 inches long strands. Bake 12–14 minutes. Allow to cool. Do this until all the dough is used up.

If you want you can fill your biscuit: Coat each cookie with jam – products such as currant jelly, orange or lemon jam work best, then cover it with a second cookie. Press gently, and then continue with the chocolate.

For the glaze, heat chocolate in a bain-marie. Cool the cookies and dip them in the chocolate. Let cool again.

Tipps

- Um helles Spritzgebäck zu backen, lassen Sie das Kakaopulver einfach weg und ersetzen die Orangenschale durch den Abrieb einer unbehandelten Zitrone.
- Spritzgebäck hält sich, in gut verschließbaren Vorratsdosen an einem kühlen Ort gelagert, über mehrere Wochen hinweg und wird mit der Zeit sogar noch mürber.

Tips & Hints

- When baking a lighter biscuit, simply leave out the cocoa powder and replace the orange zest with the grated rind of an untreated lemon.
- Biscuits keep well in a sealed storage jar in a cool place, for several weeks and matures.

WEINTALER

Zubereitungszeit inkl. Backzeit ca. 1,5 Stunden + mindestens 2 Stunden Kühlzeit

ZUTATEN

200 g Mehl
150 g kalte Butter
1 Eigelb
30 g Zucker
Abrieb von 1/2 unbehandelten Zitrone
2–3 EL trockener Weißwein

AUSSERDEM Frischhaltefolie, Mehl für die Arbeitsfläche, 1 rundes Ausstechförmchen, Backpapier, Backblech, 50 g gemahlene Mandeln, 50 g Zucker

ZUBEREITUNG

Alle Zutaten für den Teig zu einem festen, glatten Teigball kneten; dabei darauf achten, dass der Teig nicht zu lange geknetet wird, sonst wird er zu klebrig! Die Teigkugel in Frischhaltefolie wickeln und für mindestens 2 Stunden – am besten jedoch über Nacht – in den Kühlschrank legen.
Backofen auf 180 Grad vorheizen.
Mandeln und Zucker in einer Schüssel miteinander vermengen und beiseitestellen. Die Teigkugel in dicke Scheiben portionieren. Die erste Scheibe messerrückendick auf der mit Mehl bestäubten Arbeitsfläche ausrollen, während der restliche Teig, erneut in Frischhaltefolie gewickelt, im Kühlschrank zwischengelagert wird. Runde Plätzchen ausstechen und auf das mit Backpapier ausgelegte Backblech legen. Ca. 15 Minuten goldgelb backen. Nur leicht abkühlen lassen.
Die noch warmen Plätzchen vorsichtig – sie sind frisch aus dem Ofen noch sehr zerbrechlich – im Mandel-Zucker-Gemisch wälzen. Anschließend auf einer Kuchenplatte oder einem großen Teller auskühlen lassen.
Mit dem Teig weiter so verfahren, bis er gänzlich aufgebraucht ist – immer wieder im Kühlschrank zwischenlagern.

Tipps

* *Weintaler passen außerhalb der Weihnachtssaison auch gut zum Espresso oder als süßes Knabbergebäck zu Wein und Dessertweinen.*

WINE COOKIES

Preparation time including baking time approx. 1 1/2 hours + at least 2 hours cooling time

INGREDIENTS

1 3/5 cups flour
10 Tb cold butter
1 egg yolk
1/8 cup sugar
grated rind of 1/2 lemon
2–3 Tb dry white wine

IN ADDITION clear plastic wrap, flour for the work surface, 1 round cookie cutout, baking parchment, baking sheet, scant 1/4 cup ground almonds, scant 1/4 cup sugar

METHOD

Knead together all the ingredients for the dough to a smooth, firm ball. Make sure not to overknead, otherwise the dough will become too sticky. Wrap the dough in clear plastic wrap and refrigerate for at least 2 hours – if possible overnight.
Preheat oven to 350°F.
Mix the sugar and ground almonds in a bowl and set aside. Cut the ball of dough into thick slices (as if cutting pieces off a loaf of bread). On a floured work surface, roll out the first slice until the dough is 1/8 inch thick. Cover the other dough slices with clear plastic wrap again and put back in the refrigerator while not in use. Cut out round cookies and place them on a baking sheet lined with parchment. Bake for about 15 minutes until golden. Only let cool slightly.
The freshly removed cookies are still very fragile and easy to crumble – be very gentle and handle them with care. Carefully dredge cookies in the almond-sugar mixture. Place on a platter or plate to cool.
Continue the procedure – making sure to always refrigerate the unused dough – until you have used up all the dough.

Tips & Hints

* *Wine cookies can be enjoyed all year round. Serve with Espresso or coffee, or as a sweet snack to go with wine.*

ZIMTSTERNE

Zubereitungszeit inkl. Backzeit ca. 1 Stunde + mindestens 12 Stunden Ruhezeit (über Nacht)

ZUTATEN

3 Eiweiß
1 Prise Salz
250 g Puderzucker
250–300 g Mandeln, fein gemahlen
2 gehäufte TL Zimt
2 EL Zitronensaft
1/2 TL Kakaopulver

AUSSERDEM 1 sternförmiger Plätzchenausstecher, 2–3 Backbleche, Backpapier, 100 g Zucker zum Ausrollen

ZUBEREITUNG

Eiweiße mit 1 Prise Salz sehr steif schlagen. Den Puderzucker dabei während des Schlagens nach und nach dazusieben (es ist wirklich wichtig, dass der Eischnee sehr steif ist, deswegen nach dem Zufügen des Puderzuckers noch mindestens 8 Minuten auf der höchsten Stufe Ihres Rührgeräts weiter schlagen!).
2 gehäufte EL des Eischnees zum Glasieren wegnehmen und beiseitestellen. Mandeln mit Zimt, Zitronensaft und Kakaopulver mischen und unter den restlichen Schnee ziehen.
Zucker auf die Arbeitsfläche streuen und den Teig darauf etwa 5 mm dick ausrollen. Sterne ausstechen und auf die vorbereiteten Backbleche setzen, mit dem restlichen Eischnee bestreichen. Über Nacht bei Zimmertemperatur ruhen lassen.
Am Tag darauf das Backrohr auf 225 Grad vorheizen und die Zimtsterne 4–5 Minuten vorsichtig backen, darauf achten, dass sie nicht braun werden. Auf dem Blech abkühlen lassen.

Tipps

* *Der Teig braucht beim Weiterverarbeiten etwas Fingerspitzengefühl, weil er sehr klebt. Befeuchten Sie immer wieder Ihre Hände und auch das Nudelholz mit kaltem Wasser, dann lässt er sich viel besser ausrollen. Das Gleiche gilt für den Ausstecher: Spülen Sie ihn zwischendurch immer wieder unter kaltem, klarem Wasser ab, das erleichtert Ihnen die Arbeit erheblich!*
* *Wenn der Teig zu sehr klebt, einfach löffelweise gemahlene Mandeln zusätzlich zugeben, bis der Teig die richtige Konsistenz hat.*

CINNAMON STARS

Preparation time including baking time 1 hour + at least 12 hours (overnight) resting period

INGREDIENTS

3 egg whites
1 pinch salt
1 cup powdered sugar
3–3 1/2 cups almonds, finely ground
2 heaped tsp cinnamon
2 Tb lemon juice
1/2 tsp cocoa powder

IN ADDITION 1 star-shaped cookie cutter, 2–3 baking trays, baking paper, 1/2 cup sugar for rolling out

METHOD

Beat egg whites with a pinch of salt until very stiff. Gradually sieve the powdered sugar while beating the egg whites (after the addition to the powdered sugar continue beating for at least 8 minutes on the highest level of your mixer as it is really important that the egg whites are very stiff, which the Germans call "snow").
Remove 2 heaped Tb of the meringue for the icing and set aside. Mix almonds with cinnamon, lemon juice and cocoa powder and put under the remaining "snow."
Sprinkle sugar on the work surface and roll out the dough on it about 1/5 inches thick. Cut out stars and place them on the prepared baking sheets, spread the remaining beaten egg whites. Let rest at room temperature overnight.
The next day, preheat the oven to 450°F and bake the cinnamon stars carefully for 4–5 minutes. Make sure that they do not turn brown. Let cool on the sheet.

Tips & Hints

* *The dough needs some encouragement in the process because it is very sticky. Moisten your hands and the rolling pin with cold water again and again, so the dough can roll out much better. The same applies to the cutter: rinse it from time to time under cold, clear water. That makes your job easier.*
* *If the dough sticks too much, simply add some ground almonds spoon by spoon until the dough has the right consistency.*

* *Wenn Sie Ihre Zimtsterne sofort backen wollen – also auf die Ruhezeit über Nacht verzichten möchten –, können Sie sie auch gleich bei ca. 150 Grad ca. 15 Minuten im Ofen backen. Allerdings können die Sterne dann nicht allzu lange aufbewahrt werden – sie werden schneller hart.*
* *Zimtsterne halten sich, an einem kühlen Ort gelagert, mehrere Wochen lang in gut verschließbaren Vorratsdosen.*

* *If you want to bake your cinnamon star immediately – to forego the resting period overnight –, they can also be baked at about 300°F for 15 minutes in the oven. But the stars cannot be kept for long as they will quickly turn stale.*
* *Cinnamon stars, stored in a cool place, will keep for several weeks in a well-sealed storage jar.*

VANILLEKIPFERL

Zubereitungszeit inkl. Backzeit ca. 1 Stunde 20 Minuten + mindestens 2 Stunden Kühlzeit für den Teig

ZUTATEN

200 g kalte Butter
280 g Mehl
100 g geschälte, gemahlene Mandeln
40 g Vanillezucker

AUSSERDEM Frischhaltefolie, Backpapier, Backblech, Vanillezucker zum Wälzen

ZUBEREITUNG

Aus den Zutaten für den Teig einen festen, glatten Teig kneten. Die Teigkugel in Frischhaltefolie einschlagen und mindestens 2 Stunden lang – am besten jedoch über Nacht – im Kühlschrank ruhen lassen.
Den Backofen auf 200 Grad vorheizen. Die Teigkugel in ca. 1 cm dicke Scheiben schneiden. Kleine Stückchen aus dem Teig brechen und Hörnchen formen. Teig, den Sie gerade nicht benötigen, wieder in Frischhaltefolie wickeln und zurück in den Kühlschrank legen. Die Kipferl auf ein mit Backpapier ausgelegtes Backblech legen und im Ofen ca. 15–20 Minuten golden backen. So verfahren, bis der Teig aufgebraucht ist. Die fertigen Vanillekipferl noch lauwarm in Vanillezucker wälzen, damit der Zucker besser haften bleibt.

Tipp Vanillekipferl halten sich in gut verschließbaren Vorratsdosen, an einem kühlen Ort gelagert, mehrere Wochen lang.

VANILLA CRESCENT COOKIES

Preparation time including baking time approx. 1 hour 20 minutes + at least 2 hours cooling time

INGREDIENTS

14 Tb cold butter
2 cups flour
1/2 cup blanched, ground almonds
2 tsp (1 sachet) vanilla sugar

IN ADDITION clear plastic wrap, baking parchment, baking sheet, vanilla sugar for the vanilla crescents' sugar coating

METHOD

Knead the ingredients for the dough into a firm, smooth mass. Wrap the ball of dough in clear plastic wrap and refrigerate for at least 2 hours – if possible overnight.
Preheat oven to 400°F. Cut off 1/2-inch thick slices from the dough. Break off small pieces from the dough and shape into crescents. Wrap and return any unused portion of the dough to the refrigerator. Place the crescents on a baking sheet lined with parchment and bake until golden, about 15–20 minutes. Continue this procedure with the remaining dough. Dip the crescents into the sugar while still warm so that it adheres better.

Tips & Hints "Vanillekipferl" will keep for several weeks when stored in an airtight container in a cool place.

REGISTER

INDEX

LITERATURHINWEISE / REFERENCES

* »Aus dem Kochtopf der Dorfhelferinnen, Teil 2: Süße Sachen«, München o. J.
* »Bayerisches Kochbuch«, München 2007.
* Andreas Geitl: »Köstliches aus der bayerischen Küche«, Köln o. J.
* Frank Gerhard: »Kulinarische Erlebnisreise durch Bayern«, Blaufelden o. J.
* Gemeindebücherei Gmund (Hrsg.): »Kuchen und Torten. Lieblingsrezepte unserer Leser«, Gmund am Tegernsee 2011.
* »Guats mit Äpfel. Backrezepte aus der Pfarrei Gmund am Tegernsee«, Gmund am Tegernsee 2006.
* Annemarie Köllerer: »Bayerisches Schmankerlbuch«, Dachau o. J.
* Olli Leeb: »Bayerische Leibspeisen«, München o. J.
* »Das Milchkochbuch«, München 2009.
* Susanne Seethaler: »Die echte bayerische Küche. Traditional Bavarian Cooking«, München 2005.
* Susanne Seethaler: »Vom Glück, mit Liebe zu kochen«, München 2010.

DANK

Mein Dank geht an alle leidenschaftlichen Bäcker und Bäckerinnen, die mir ihre Rezepte und Backtricks für dieses Buch verraten haben: Annette Borkenhagen, Rosi Köstler, Ines Stöhr (Gartensalon, München), Irmgard Seethaler, Irmgard Stiegeler, Gabi Klein, Burgi, Pfarrer Wernberger und Suzy Seelings Vater Peter.
Meiner Freundin Maria Bachmann danke ich für ihren Beistand in meiner Küche und Katharina, die zuweilen als Vorkosterin fungierte, für ihre begeisterten Kommentare zu unseren Kreationen.
Und ich danke meinen Mädels aus dem Gartensalon: »Gastronomie ist ja eigentlich kein Zuckerschlecken!«, aber mit euch am Herd und im Laden zu stehen, das ist einfach nur genial!
Ein ganz spezielles Dankeschön geht zum Schluss noch an den amerikanischen Zen-Koch Edward Espe Brown und seinen Partner Ponce, die über die letzten Jahre hinweg meine Freunde geworden sind.

ACKNOWLEDGMENTS

I wish to thank those passionate bakers, who have shared their recipes, tips, tricks and secrets with me while writing this book: Annette Borkenhagen, Rosi Köstler, Ines Stöhr (Gartensalon, München), Irmgard Seethaler, Irmgard Stiegeler, Gabi Klein, Burgi, Reverend Wernberger and Suzy Seeling's father Peter.
Many thanks to my friend Maria Bachmann for standing by me in my kitchen studio and Katharina, who, while often performing taste tests, provided enthusiastic comments thus encouraging my culinary experiments.

And, of course, I want to thank all my girls at the Gartensalon: although "the restaurant business is not a piece of cake," working with you all in the kitchen and at the store was wonderful, if not in fact sweet.
In closing, a special thanks to the Zen chef Edward Espe Brown and his partner Ponce, who have become my friends over the years.

DIE AUTORIN

Susanne Seethaler, geboren 1969, wuchs am oberbayerischen Tegernsee auf. Vor mehr als zehn Jahren begann sie, Bücher über ihre bayerische Heimat zu schreiben. Auf ihren vielen Reisen findet sie Inspirationen und Ideen für neue Buchthemen. Aber gerade ihre Liebe zu den Schönheiten und Eigenarten Bayerns hat sie zum Schreiben bewogen. Neben traumhaften Landschaften und ungewöhnlichen, mystischen Geschichten gilt ihr Interesse vor allem altem, überliefertem Wissen, das es zu bewahren gilt, bevor es dem Vergessen anheimfällt. 1999 erschien ihr Buch »Sagenhafte Burgen und Schlösser in Oberbayern«, 2003 »Altbayerische Klöster und Legenden«, 2004 »Unsere bayerische Lebensart«, 2005 »Die echte bayerische Küche. Traditional Bavarian Cooking«, 2007 »Das Heilwissen der Bauern«, 2009 »Das Heilwissen der Frauen vom Land« und 2010 »Vom Glück, mit Liebe zu kochen«.
Susanne Seethaler kocht regelmäßig in einem Münchner Café und gibt landesweit Workshops zum Thema Achtsamkeit in der Küche. Sie lebt, schreibt und kocht in München.

THE AUTHOR

Born in 1969 and raised in the idyllic Tegernsee lakes region nestled in a valley near the mountains, Susanne Seethaler began writing books about her Bavarian homeland more than a decade ago. In search of inspiration for new subjects, she started traveling widely throughout the world. Her love of the beauty and unique features of Bavaria moved her to write. In addition to lovely landscapes and unusual, mystical stories, her interest is mostly old, traditional knowledge, worth preserving before it falls into oblivion. Her book "Fabulous Castles and Palaces in Bavaria" was published in 1999, in 2003 "Bavarian Monasteries and Legends," in 2004 "Our Bavarian Way of Life," in 2005 "Real Bavarian Cuisine. Traditional Bavarian Cooking." "The Healing Wisdom of Farmers" appeared in 2007 followed in 2009 by "The Healing Wisdom of Country Women." "Cooking with Love leads to Happiness" was published in 2010.
Susanne Seethaler cooks regularly in a Munich Café and gives workshops on mindfulness in the kitchen across the country. She lives, writes, and cooks in Munich.

Lassen Sie sich verführen:
Die besten Rezepte der bayerischen Küche!

Here they are:
treasures of traditional Bavarian cooking!